Learn To Lead

Author
Rajesh Sachdev

BlueRose ONE
Stories Matter
New Delhi • London

BLUEROSE PUBLISHERS
India | U.K.

For permissions requests or inquiries regarding this publication,
please contact:

BLUEROSE PUBLISHERS
www.BlueRoseONE.com
info@bluerosepublishers.com
+91 8882 898 898
+4407342408967

ISBN: 978-93-6452-392-9

First Edition: June 2024

Being an excellent individual contributor does not automatically qualify one to be an effective leader. Leadership is a distinct skill set that requires training & development.

How can an individual who excelled in their field, suddenly face challenges when asked to lead others?

- Top Performer promoted as a team leader
- Stumbles when promoted to a leadership role
- Team satisfaction and output goes down
- Founds himself torn between his team and his higher-ups
- Struggles to keep everyone happy but ending up satisfying no one.

Transform Your LEADERS With ALL ABOUT LEADING Programs

Transformation Approach

- Insight
- Assessment
- Training
- Application
- Coaching

- Improves skills to lead people
- Leads team in a better way
- Increases team productivity & satisfaction
- Improves Overall Growth of the Organization
- Financial Benefits because of better output and lower

More than 20 Times ROI (Financial benefits in crores of rupees) because of increase in team output and low attrition

I dedicate this book to all my readers who possess Courage to transform their leadership skills and strive to become the best versions of themselves. Your willingness to change and improve inspires me deeply. I feel honoured to share my experiences and principles with you, and through this book, I hope to give back to society in meaningful ways.

My deepest gratitude to Devna Mishra for her invaluable assistance in articulating my thoughts and shaping this book.

Contents

P Preface

With my 30 years of corporate experience, I was fortunate enough to engage in leadership roles that gave me a fresh new understanding of becoming a better leader. My undying passion was to give back to society through the learnings that I had accumulated.
To fulfil my passion, I planned to become a full-time facilitator for leadership development and coaching.

After deep analysis and study, I quickly realised that there was a set of must-have skills for anyone and everyone to be a good leader. It was then that I integrated all my knowledge and experience in a structured manner to effectively imbibe and enhance their abilities by enabling them with the missing ingredients to become a great leader.

I wanted to fill the gaps that were amiss, and this led me to create fine guidelines that were easy to adapt and execute. This is when I decided to write this book and create leadership development programs that not only had twists and turns but were fun yet technically appropriate. And, after all, what is knowledge, if not shared!

The leaders, after reading this book, will be enriched and come to understand the common and minimalistic gaps that they were oblivious to. The contents of this book are designed to ascertain that the knowledge and the tools mentioned in the book, will help them in every sphere of their lives.

This endeavour of mine will serve as a handbook and a hand-holder for participants and audience for leadership development programs. For this specific audience, I have shared details of modules in the beginning of the book. While, for readers who are not participants of the training, they should treat these four modules as four sections of the book.

MODULE

01

Getting Ready for the Change

I normally call this module ZEROTH MODULE as this is the base of all that we will learn in this program. It has following components.

- The Golden Rule: Being Ethical
- Decode Your Mind – A basic tool to zoom in to understand yours and other's thoughts/actions
- Insight - Difference between a manager and a leader
- Get Ready for Change – Change is the only constant
- Power of positive thinking
- The winning spirit and self-motivation
- Power of mindfulness activities

You can get an in-depth understanding of the above-mentioned components in the following chapters.

The first two topics improve the basic skills and qualities of participants.

The topic (difference between manager and leader) gives you an eye-opening insight into what a good leader looks like, and this sets your expectations for what changes you are going to bring after the program is over.

Now you know what change you want to bring in. I would like to give more insight on how you can prepare for the change and keep yourselves motivated during the whole program.

"Trust is the byproduct of ethics and integrity"

MODULE 02

Amplify your effectiveness with Emotional Intelligence

Why do smart people fail? Why do technically brilliant individuals have trouble managing others and collaborating on a team? What distinguishes great leaders from merely good ones? It isn't IQ or technical skills, says Daniel Goleman. It's Emotional Intelligence: a group of skills that enable the best leaders to maximize their own and their followers' performance. The five components of EI which are:

1. Self-awareness
2. Self-regulation
3. Motivation
4. Empathy
5. Social Skill

You can read more about EI and its importance in the chapters (EMOTIONAL INTELLIGENCE (EI))

The module covers the following topics

- Understand what emotional intelligence is
- Learn tools to build emotional intelligence
- Power of being non-judgmental and tools how to build it.
- Difference between Observation Vs Judgmental and Thinking Vs Feeling.
- ICEBERG- Tool to understand your emotions
- OAR (Observe, Action, Result) framework to fix your actions for the best result
- Different Body Dispositions (Resolution, Flexibility, Stability, and Openness)

"Emotional Intelligence is the key to both personal and professional success"

MODULE 03

Different Leadership Styles: Tailor it to fit your people

We cover the following topics in this module:

- Different leadership styles and how they are different from each other
- How each style deliberately influences the different factors (like flexibility, responsibility, etc.) of an organization.
- Situation Based Leadership
- Skill-Will Matrix
- Demotivating factors are different from the factor which motivates them
- Motivate people with more responsibility rather than money

This training programs talks about different leadership styles used by various leaders.

1) **Coercive** Leaders demand immediate compliance
2) **Authoritative** leaders mobilize people toward a vision.
3) **Affiliative** Leaders create emotional bonds and harmony
4) **Democratic** Leaders build consensus through participation
5) **Pacesetting** leaders expect excellence and self-direction
6) **Coaching** leaders develop people for the future

After discussing different styles, we discuss about Situation based Leadership and different body dispositions and then details how we can motivate our team members.

"Leadership is the Process of Getting Everyone to the Place They are Supposed to Go"

MODULE 04

Communication Skills & Essential Tools for a Good Leader

"Nothing in life is more important than the ability to communicate effectively.

"If you just communicate, you can get by. But if you communicate skilfully, you can work miracles."

"To effectively communicate, we must realize that we are all different in the way we perceive the world and use this understanding as a guide to our communication with others."

"Excellent communication doesn't just happen naturally. It is a product of process, skill, climate, relationship and hard work."

"Communication works for those who work at it."

The above quotes explain the importance of communication skill and why should we work on it. The topics covered in this module are:

- Sharpen your communication skills.
    - Work on listening & asking more than telling
    - Work on being non-judgmental, separating out feelings from thoughts and requesting need instead of demanding strategy.
- Active Listening
- GROW Model (Asking)
- Telling - Setting SMART Goals
- Telling - Sharing Feedback (REACH Model))
- Share your Gratitude – A Great tool to strengthen relationship
- Conflict Management
- Negotiation Skills & How to Say No

"Great leaders communicate and great communicators lead"

CHAPTER 01

Change is the only Constant

"The ability to adapt to change, determines your success"

There's a fantastic saying: "Change is the only constant in life." This timeless truth is something we can't deny or escape. Trust me, when I tell you that change always guides us towards opportunities: this reality resonates in every aspect of our lives—whether its entering into a marriage venturing, or into the thrilling world of starting a business or experiencing the emotional moment of witnessing your child take their first steps. Each of these moments opens up possibilities for us to explore. Just picture the mix of emotions when you see your child off to college or the heartwarming joy of bringing a pet who quickly becomes part of your family. The changes that life brings whether big or small introduce us to joys and obstacles pushing us to evolve and embrace all aspects of being human.

In a nutshell, 'CHANGES, GENERALLY ARE FOR SOMETHING GOOD.'

Now let me introduce you to my first protagonist, Dev as we dive into the corporate world.

Imagine you've just aced the dream project of your career. Your heart swells with pride. You are at the top of your game, the star player everyone cheers for. Then almost overnight, you're stepping into a new role. No longer just a team member, but the team leader. How amazing is that?

Yes, the above is Dev's story! It is just a glimpse of Dev's professional accomplishments. Based on his performance in Sales responsibility, he is promoted as Sales Regional Head, where he is supposed to lead team of around 20 People.

Understandably, he rejoiced, had his fair share of celebrations, and is now eager to take on his new role. There was nothing in Dev's life that was amiss. But there is so much more that he achieved. We will get to those enticing details, soon.

Now let us see the flipside of Dev's journey. As he was stepping ahead in making his life a complete panorama of a wholesome world, he got stuck! His validated assumption of becoming the Regional Sales Head got shattered. Yes, he stepped into the new role, made some incredible achievements that were beneficial for his company and for him, but it didn't last, and understandably enough, his previous position was at stake, right?

What was it that could possibly have gone wrong?
What do you all perceive of it?

The answers popping up in your head right now will be numerous, but the fact that I want to put across and get you people thinking is simply: **'DO YOU NEED TO GET READY; READY FOR THE CHANGE?'**
My answer to the above is a resounding, **YES!**

Before we move ahead with Dev's story, let me share the message that I want to bring to light through this chapter.

A leader should be proactive and tackle challenges directly. This chapter will prepare you to confidently face and overcome any obstacle that arises. It can be professional or personal, technical, or adaptive. And along the same lines, I will align you with the changes that have to be worked upon for the leadership role.

Just like in the narrative of the book "Who Moved My Cheese", we encounter various characters that each one of us can identify with. Some of us are Sniffs who detect change early and take proactive steps to adapt. Others are Scurry's who take swift action, or Hems, who resist and fear change. And then there are the Haws, who learn to adapt in time when they see the benefit of change.

These characters don't just live in stories. They are archetypes representing a varied responses to change. Identifying with one can be both enlightening and empowering. It prompts a question with profound implications. Which character are you? But more importantly, which character do you aspire to be?

All Dev's are amongst one of the above characters.
Now, let's check out what was the mindset of our Dev. He was a replica of Hems & Haws who believed in handling things as they come. Dev was known for his laid-back approach, often handling situations as they arose. He doesn't burden himself with excessive planning or worry about the future. Instead, he prefers to tackle challenges at the moment they occur, trusting in his ability to adapt and respond effectively to whatever comes his way. However, this method often led to hurdles and challenges, as it meant that he was unprepared for foreseeable changes.

What clearly happened in such a situation, Dev lost everything. Apart from the assets and the recognition, his position as a team leader where he had started his glittering journey, collapsed! Yes, he failed. The cheese that he so relished, went in the bin.

Conversely, the other two mice (Sniff and Scurry) have distinctly different approach towards life. Here, I would like to introduce my second protagonist, Jay. He is someone who showcases a meticulous and structured approach to navigating his environment. He epitomizes careful planning and anticipation. He embraced the change without fear, willingly took risks, and actively prepared himself for upcoming changes. This cautious demeanour stems from a desire to maintain security and avoid the unknown, reflecting a deep-seated resistance to change.

Jay's journey through the maze is a testament to the challenges that come with a fixed mindset, emphasizing the importance of adaptability and openness to new experiences as old certainties disappear. And the aroma and flavour of fresh cheese that Jay patiently waited for, would exhilarate not just his taste buds, but his life as a whole.

So, let us embrace and work toward the only constant, i.e., 'CHANGE', because...

So far, we have learned and understood that change is the only constant and it is inevitable. Change is beneficial and beautiful, and we must be prepared for it. The quicker we adapt to change, the better the outcomes would be.

"Change is Hard at first, Messy in the middle and Gorgeous at the end"

Getting Ready for Change (How this book is going to help you)
Along the way I will help all the Dev's out there to be the Jays that they can be. All they need is a guide, a mentor, who can bring out the characteristics of Jay that they too have but are oblivious of them. That's where I will help you through this book.

The next crucial things to consider are,

Does new leadership role demand new skills?
Are you ready, for a shift, for a change?
Are you ready to be a great leader?

If you are still uncertain, then be ready for tasting the stale cheese that could have been as fresh as you would have wanted it to be. What you'll get out of non-acceptance are many more failures that will lead you to bury the thought of being a leader. My intent is not do discourage you: it is simply unpreventable!

But, if your response is yes, then let's start this journey together. It might not be a ride. It will, undoubtedly lead you towards personal satisfaction and help mould you into a leader. This journey will push your limits, test your abilities, and ultimately provide you with the expertise, necessary to guide and motivate others. While navigating through this expedition, you'll uncover strengths within yourself.

It's time to create a future that aligns perfectly with your dreams. There will be ups and downs during this voyage but in the end, they will be worth it!

In the upcoming sections on change, we'll explore two key areas. First, we'll discuss why people often struggle with change. Understanding the common obstacles and fears can help us address them effectively. Second, we'll examine how to transform any change into a beneficial opportunity. By accepting change, we can open new opportunities and achieve greater success.

Why do people fail?

It's a common understanding that any final product undergoes several stages of transformation. Take a mango shake, for example: the mango must first be peeled and chopped, then blended with milk—a completely different ingredient. Through this process, the mango changes form and character, but it ultimately enhances the shake with its rich flavour.

Similarly, when we humans decide to tread on the path to 'change', there will be transformations.

There are stages one goes through on the journey, towards self-improvement and leadership each presenting its unique challenges. It's crucial for those aiming to lead in any field to understand and navigate these stages effectively to tackle the obstacles they bring.

The common reasons for people failing / facing tough challenges for these changes are Lack of Vision, sticking with comfort zone, resistance, lack of persistence, and more.

Initially many individuals may not realize the need for change sticking to their routines until something triggers a realization of growth. Moving beyond the comfort zone of familiarity comes next once the need for change is acknowledged. During this time, it's crucial to avoid falling back into old ways of thinking and acting, especially when new leadership challenges arise. This often brings about feelings of doubt and uneasiness fuelled by fear of not meeting expectations or lacking the skills and resources for success.

One significant hurdle that can arise throughout these stages is procrastination, driven by a mix of anxiety and a desire for comfort leading to delays in making efforts, towards change.

Successfully handling these changes is essential for developing resilience and skills needed to manage change effectively. By facing/accepting these challenges, individuals can use their strengths to adapt and grow. This empowers them to accept change and make a positive impact in various areas of life.

My dear readers I hope I did not scare you too much. Yes, it may seem daunting in the beginning, but trust-you-me, it's the most rewarding and fulfilling feeling that you will ever experience.

How to turn any change into a fruitful outcome or opportunity?
In this section, I will explore **how you can turn any change into a fruitful outcome or opportunity.** We'll look at strategies for leveraging change to your advantage, ensuring that you can make the most out of new situations and challenges.

Ok, let's hop on to a little exercise here.

"Does every change come with a new opportunity, or does a new opportunity always bring change?"

Reflect on the significant changes that have occurred in your life. And here I am not referring to any one aspect of your life, but a general way:

1. When you experienced the change, was it painful initially?
2. Do you believe those changes were avoidable?
3. Given that there were no other options, how were you able to cope with this change?
4. How do you feel now, looking back at those changes?

My sole intention to make you reflect on all the above questions was to make you realise that the change was inevitable. It was and is a part of the process. It could or must have been tormenting and you may have thought of quitting it all, but you hung on, pushed yourself to the edge, and things changed in your favour.

Now think about that one big change that you enjoyed in the period of change. What was the difference in your demeanour,

and the impact on your life at that time as compared to other changes?
Let me take the privilege of answering the question. Because I feel that most of you will agree.

The change in attitude was most noticeable during that one major transition that was welcomed with open arms. Instead of fear or opposition, there was an atmosphere of interest and anticipation. With an optimistic outlook, not only was the change easier, but the advantages were magnified, turning difficulties into chances for personal development. The effect on one's life was significant; what may have been a stressful moment turned into an exciting opportunity for growth and discovery. In this way, we saw how a positive attitude towards change can transform the experience, transforming possible challenges into opportunities for growth in our careers and lives.

The key lesson here is that change is always for the better. We should embrace it with confidence, knowing that it leads to positive improvements. By accepting that situations will improve with change, we can approach new opportunities with optimism and readiness to succeed. This mindset ensures that we view each change as a step towards a better future.

Another point is that to be part of the change and enjoy it, one must have faith in the process. This faith can be based on the concept that 'I can deal with the change. Every day will change; whether it is good or bad, it will change.' Alternatively, it can be the belief that something unasked for is a gift from God, and God's gifts are always for the good.

You might be feeling that I am getting religious/spiritual. But understand, incorporating a spiritual understanding into leadership is essential, as it brings a deeper dimension to guiding others and making decisions. This isn't about a 'spiritual leader' per se but about recognising the subtle yet powerful influence of spiritual awareness in leadership roles. Such awareness can foster a more profound respect for diversity, and a commitment to ethics. This holistic approach to problem-solving is an added asset.

Let's return to the point I was making about using faith as a tool to ease your journey through change.

Emphasising faith in the context means having confidence in the unseen, the potential within each situation and person. It encourages leaders to approach challenges with optimism and trust in the positive outcomes of their decisions. It is these decisions or thought processes that leave the desired impact on another individual. My dear readers, aspiring leaders, and future guides, faith is one of the most essential attributes as far your belief goes.

The conviction in "faith" carves a path that leads you to your desired goals. Having faith in the fact that the 'change' will be nothing but the 'best.' If you are in acceptance of this then your road to success is undeniably the one that others would love to explore. A true leader only intent is to change the lives of all the Dev's out there, pull them out of the thought of 'impossible' to 'I'm possible.'

Now all you need to do is reflect upon the fact that whether "your intention," is in place and crystal clear or not! Are you ready to take the plunge? Do you affirm that yes, 'I embrace the change with all the pitfalls and hurdles', because I want to be that light at the end of the tunnel for all those who have given up!

And let me tell you that my 'faith' in the leaders of tomorrow who are reading this book, will join me in exploring the skills that shall be revealed in the coming chapters. So, pull the pin, unplug and get in sync with my mantra as a leader, "the sky is not the limit!'

Let's summarize here, Success is just around the corner—always remember that change is a consistent part of life, bringing new opportunities to fulfil our dreams and enhance the lives of others. Accept change positively, because it's a natural progression. You possess the qualities needed to turn challenges into opportunities for growth and to carve out your own path to success. Have faith and do what is necessary; you may receive benefits from the change that you never even imagined.

"Fear not of exploring the unknown, for it is there that discovery awaits."
– Rajesh Sachdev

Keep reading...

CHAPTER 02

The Golden Rule: Being Ethical

"Management is doing things right, Leadership is doing the right things"

And here I would like to bring Dev back into the picture. Despite the fact that he witnessed ups and downs in his career, but there was one beautiful element that cannot be denied and that was the love and respect he had earned from his team. They were not just his supporters, but also admired him and looked up to him in any big or small work situations. They knew that their team leader was the one person on whom they could fully depend upon. Be it any time of the day or night, if any team member/members got stuck, Dev was just a phone call away.

The team would be all pepped-up and high on spirits to come to office every single day because Dev was a force who inspired them and gave them that dignity and appreciation of being special in their own respective ways. They felt secured and wanted. His teammates were, indeed, his biggest supporters. The manner in which the team performed it was like no looking back. It was all about moving ahead for a brighter future. The team flourished with the encouragement and support they received from their leader. Their dedication went beyond benefiting the organization; it was fuelled by a feeling of being part of something meaningful driven by their leader's strong work ethic. As they pushed forward together it became evident that, through unity and motivational leadership progress, for both individuals and the organization was certain guiding the company towards success.

But do you know why was this so?

Why did Dev's team have this level of respect towards him?

Why was it that the team always delivered far better than what was expected out of them?

Well, let me tell you.

Dev's Strong work ethic was the core reason his team held him in such high regard and consistently outperformed expectations he led by example showing integrity, accountability and fairness in every action and interaction. This built a deep trust and respect among his teammates. He also made it a point to recognize and value each team members unique contributions this not only boosted morale but also motivated everyone to surpass their targets driven by a desire to meet the high standards their leaders set.

Dev's approach turned the workplace into a dynamic environment where professional growth and personal respect were intertwined. The team didn't just work to meet objectives they were inspired to excel feeling genuinely valued and empowered under this guidance. This commitment to ethical leadership was a real secret to their sustained success and loyalty.

From this content and other sources along with my own experience in managing people I've learned a lot about effective leadership. A key insight is that any leadership strategy only works if your team has trust in you and to earn this trust you must uphold strong ethics. Simply put, without ethics, you cannot secure your team's trust and they will not fully engage with your guidance causing your efforts to fall short. Therefore,

The golden rule is: "***BE ETHICAL***"

Let's discuss this in more detail.

"Ethics is knowing the difference between what you have a right to do and what is right to do"

(नैतिकता यह नहीं है कि आपके पास क्या करने का अधिकार है बल्कि क्या करना सही है)

The golden rule has been referred to as that philosophy for leading one's life that suggests that other people should be treated fairly and with respect. We must introspect whether the decision will make us feel proud because a leader must be at peace with him or herself before taking any decision. That resolve can be related to a company policy. The leader will have to weigh the pros and cons, ethics and non-ethics, feasibility and practicality, and check for any violations of laws. And most importantly, will it be fair to all the team members both, in the long term and short-term. A leader without ethics is like a ship without a rudder, directionless and unable to steer.

"What goes around comes around/what you sow shall you reap"

(जैसा बोओगे वैसा पाओगे)

In order to create that perfect dish, you need to add all the ingredients in perfect ratio and order, else the outcome can be disastrous. In a similar way, we ought to create a concoction of all the essential characteristics to an appropriate degree in order to emerge as individuals/leaders that we always aspired to be. Goodness reaps goodness just how malice shall reap malice. Your team will be a reflection of the decisions and contributions you make. Your actions will derive equal and opposite reactions. A happy, content, and satisfied team is the outcome of that leader who has the ability to carve the statues with precision, respect, and love. All this will come back to you if there is consistency in the purity of your thoughts, words, and actions.

Moving on, another crucial quality of a true leader is honesty.

"Honesty is the best policy"

(ईमानदारी सर्वोत्तम नीति है)

When we say that honesty is the best policy, then it is in relation to aspects pertaining to being honest to yourself first. Truthfulness, morality, and righteousness are of extreme importance when we make honesty not just as a tool but as the main attribute that defines our core characteristic. An honest individual will have immense gratitude and the ability to be courteous towards others. He/she will always be able to create rather than destroy. This creation will comprise of those set of people who will have righteousness towards their work and towards their organization. When there is so much integrity in people, it is impossible that they would ever fail as individuals/leaders.

Building on this, when individuals embody honesty, they cultivate trust and respect around them. This not only enhances their own character but also positively influences their interactions. Such honesty inspires teams and organizations to adopt similar values, ethical foundation that fosters lasting achievements.

Have you ever thought about how trust and leadership are closely linked? Can a leader succeed without the trust of their team?

Imagine an office buzzing with activity where a team works under a highly experienced and skilled leader. This leader has a clear vision for the team's future. However, something is missing. The team respects the leader but doesn't fully trust them. Consequently, they often ignore instructions, and projects don't meet their goals.

This highlights the essential role of trust in leadership. Without it, even the most competent leader struggle to motivate their team and achieve goals trust is fundamentally important for effective leadership. Trustworthy leaders are those who practice ethical behaviour consistently. A leader who lacks ethics will find it hard to earn their team's trust, reducing their effectiveness the core rule of leadership is therefore to maintain ethical standards.

So, how does a leader build trust?

1. **Start by trusting your team members:** Trust in leadership works both ways. To receive trust, you must first extend it to your team
2. **Always fulfil your commitments:** Breaking promises can quickly destroy trust showing that you are reliable strengthens your team's trust in you.
3. **Recognize and appreciate your team's efforts:** A supportive environment where contributions are acknowledged build stronger trust.
4. **Focus on the team and the organizations goals rather than personal gains:** Leaders who prioritize their team and organizational objectives over their own are more likely to gain their team's trust.

What are the benefits of being ethical?

- **Strong work ethics:** Dev's leadership is deeply rooted in ethics and fairness which foster trust and admiration among his team members
- **Readiness and support:** They've consistently available offering support whenever his team needs it which enhances their cohesion and motivation.
- **Enhanced performance:** The strong bond between Dev and his team boasts both individual and organizational performance
- **Respectful workplace:** Dev's leadership creates a workplace environment where professional growth and respect are paramount.

- **Sustained success:** Ethical leadership as demonstrated by Dev is crucial for driving a team toward long term success.

Trust is vital for effective leadership and is founded on ethical behaviour it grows through actions that show dependability recognition of team efforts and prioritizing the collective goals over personal interests following the golden rule of being ethical will help build and maintain this trust.

A leader's ethical behaviour truly embodies the saying, what goes around comes around," When leaders act with integrity and fairness, they create a positive cycle of trust and respect. This positive influence circles back, leading them to loyalty, motivation, and success. By fostering an environment where ethics guide every decision, leaders not only uplift their teams but also set the stage for enduring achievements. Thus, ethical leadership not only sends out good into the world, but it also ensures that good returns, strengthening the entire organization.

As discussed above trust is the cornerstone of any successful team. Leaders must demonstrate that building and maintaining trust requires consistent efforts and ethical behaviour. Here's a simple guide on the doors and don'ts for trust building among team leaders and members:

Do's	Don'ts
Trust your team members – It is a reciprocal relationship	Don't withhold trust; it discourages openness

Do's	Don'ts
Meet your commitments to set a reliable example	Don't make promises you can't keep
Be selfless and give credit to your team members	Don't take credit of others' work
Prioritize the team's and orgnaization's needs over personal ambitions.	Don't put personal goals before the team's success
Support your team during tough time	Don't distance yourself when challenge arise
Listen actively and encourage open communication	Don't ignore or dismiss the team members' inputs

CHAPTER 03

Decode Your Mind (Deep-Diving Skill)

"Its always the small pieces that makes the big picture"

I have always been intrigued to get the answer from different people of equally diverse backgrounds, "Do we humans have free will or are we programmed by society?"

When a child is born, there are only a very few ways he/she expresses happiness, sadness, discomfort, or even love. Some cry softly, while others wail as if all hell has broken loose!! When their tummies are full/when they have had a good night's sleep their eyes radiate a gleam of utter satisfaction and absolute, untainted affection to whomsoever looks at them. So apparently, there are only a few actions, that we can literally count on our fingertips, that define a child's need for expression. But slowly and steadily they begin to pick up and adapt various other actions, sounds, expressions that they were completely oblivious of in the first few months of their lives. This goes on to indicate rather significantly that we are predominantly programmed by society. Therefore, in order to thoroughly understand human or individual behaviours, we need to "Decode the programming done by society!"

The many layers that an individual is covered with are actually gifts from society. What comes to light is that there is a set pattern in everything we do in our day-to-day life. This pattern, which I refer to as a flowchart or code, is created by society. A flowchart is a term often used in programming language. It breaks down an activity into various levels or stages, or in simpler words, it is a step-by-step progression towards completing a task.

We perform most of our daily tasks with steps embedded in our subconscious mind. Identifying these steps in detail with our conscious mind is what I refer to as “decoding your mind.”

I also call this process "drilling down" or "deep diving" into your mind. The deep-diving concept emphasizes an individual's ability to break their behavioural attributes into smaller fragments. This skill will enrich us with an understanding of why we behave or act the way we do and will enable us to transform and become the best possible versions of ourselves.

It is difficult to read second person mind, this philosophy helps you to read second person mind. This is based on the concept that in a given situation, everyone works the same way. You might say here that people behave differently, I agree with you, they behave differently because the situation (current / past) is different for different people. Coming back to the concept here, in order to understand others, lets first decode your mind, how it behaves in different situations

Let’s take the example of listing down the steps needed to make a cup of tea

1) Take a pan and put half cup of water
2) Put the pan on the gas and ignite it
3) Put half teaspoon sugar, half teaspoon tea leaves and half cup of milk
4) Wait till you see bubbles coming out from pan.
5) Boil the tea for 1 minutes (boil it till come top, then slow down the gas to get it settle. Do it 10 times)
6) Now filter it out in the cup.

We need to even think to the level whether we first put water in the pan and put it on gas first or we light the gas and then put the pan and the water?

Another Example:
Ever wondered what protocol should be chosen to cross a busy road?!
We all know that before crossing a road, we need to look left and right, but even in this seemingly simple task, the flowchart gets into the action, and each of us exhibits something indifferent, or is it somewhat similar? The steps that we take or the action that we perform is unique in their own way.

If I ask you what all you consider while crossing the road, you may share the following inputs:

- Distance of the vehicle
- Speed of the vehicle
- Your estimated speed
- Width of the road

In my opinion, there are a few more parameters that we look at while crossing the road. They are in your sub-conscious mind but if I ask you to pen down them, you might not be able to share all. Try to think how many points you are able to think of?
Let me share these points:

- The lane in which the vehicle is approaching
- The width & weight of the vehicle
- Weather
- Road conditions
- Day/Night
- The weight on our shoulders
- Alone or with Someone

And last but not the least, on a lighter note, we do take a peep as to whether it's a male, female, or a youngster at the driver's seat! Yes, you too do the same, don't you?

The drill down approach helps us to zoom in on details that are often overlooked providing a much clearer picture of the behaviours and circumstances we encounter.

HOW DOES A DRILL DOWN APPROACH HELP?

- **Deep-Dive into context:** Imagine a situation where two employees react defensively to feedback. At first glance, their reactions might seem identical. However, by using the drill down approach, our leader might discover one employee feels overwhelmed due to personal stress while the other might lack understanding of the feedback intent. Recognizing these nuances allows for tailored responses that address the true underlying issues
- **Adapting to leadership challenges:** consider a project team facing delays. The initial impression might be that the team is inefficient. However, by deep-diving, a leader might find that the delay is due to a few team members needing additional training not a lack of effort. This insight shifts the response from frustration to one of support and development.
- **Exploring rather than judging:** for example, a leader notices that an employee often misses morning meetings. Instead of judging them for being unprofessional the drill down approach would encourage the leader to explore. It might turn out that the employee has recently become a parent and is adjusting to a new schedule, Pointing to a need for flexibility rather than discipline.

These examples highlight how the drill down approach allows leaders to understand the specific contexts and complexities of each situation. This understanding leads to more effective leadership, where decisions are not, No one's understanding of the factors influencing behaviour, responsive, and ultimately, a successful environment.

Therefore, it depends on our sets of skills and abilities, how minutely we can conceive a detailed breakage in our minds. It automatically becomes relevant and clear that with this potential of breaking the flowchart into tiny fragments, we are definitely in a better situation to understand human behaviours, in general. We are equipped with the understanding of how far, wide and intricately, can the human mind function.

Not only can we understand our own minds and our emotions, but we discharge a unique potential that enables us to be all the more empathetic towards others too.

Many interesting aspects begin to come to light once we are able to decode this flowchart which is different with each and every individual. One of them being, that we are able to understand and reflect upon the many scenarios and varied backgrounds, for that particular outcome or end-product. This would lead us to the position of being able to identify with that specific individual, in all areas. Because the final outcome is a reflection of the inner personality of that one particular and peculiar human being. We also get to know:

1. Is the action intentional?
2. Is there a lethargy or a laid-back approach?
3. Is there an element of procrastination?
4. Is it that the individual has put in a100% effort, yet the results are not up to the mark?

If we explore, we will find that there can be innumerable reasons for such an outcome. These reasons will determine our course of action, or our approach towards the individual. We would have to contemplate, after studying the flowchart, whether he/she needs to be reprimanded or a totally opposite strategy will have to be applied, in order to come to the bottom of the situation.

Let's consider a simple example to illustrate this point. Imagine an employee named Alex, who is usually very diligent and meets his sales targets. However, this month, Alex's performance has dipped, and he hasn't met his usual standards. On the surface, it might seem like Alex didn't put in enough effort. But if we apply the drill down approach, we might discover various underlying factors contributing to his performance. Upon closer examination we might find that Alex was tasked with using a new sales software that he hasn't fully mastered yet or perhaps he was dealing with some temporary personal issues that affected his focus at work.

The deep diving (an in depth understanding) helps us determine whether Alex's situation warrants a supportive response rather than a punitive one. For instance, if the issue is with the new software perhaps the additional training is required if personal issues are distracting him, may be some flexible work arrangements could help him regain his focus stop

This approach avoids a one-size-fits-all reaction and instead tailor's actions to the specific circumstances of each individual, acknowledging that even a committed employee might face hurdles that affect their output. This thoughtful consideration helps maintain motivation and support for continuous improvement demonstrating compassionate and effective leadership.

Whatever we do in day-to-day life, it has a kind of set-of-instructions that we follow, and it is something programmed by the society based on our experiences. We are so

much into following these instructions, that we never see them at a minute level. The DYM tool has explained how you can visualize these tasks into smaller fragments or in other words zoom out the situation at hand and check the list of activities we perform in order to attain victory over it. The breakdown into smaller chunks, I call this, 'The drilldown approach'.

It is not easy, neither is it difficult to drilldown your actions into smaller unambiguous tasks. All you would need is a clear and crisp thought pattern. If practiced religiously, this ability to break down any given situation into little parts, would aid you to carefully align the set of instructions in your flowchart. And once this is accomplished, no task will ever turn out anything, except how you wanted it!

Once you have practised drilling down everything, you will realize, that you upfront can read your behaviour and not just your own mind, you will be able to read another person's mind also. To read another person's mind, you must put yourself in another person's place to see how your flowchart works in that scenario. If you are able to identify what's there in another person mind up to 70-80% that's a big step towards reading another person mind.

There is a proverb (बाल की खाल निकालना) which means viewing the things minutely. Although it is used in more negative sense for arguing about something which is not important or case when someone is trying to introduce a quibble. But if you relate this proverb, it is almost same what we are doing by DYM-Drill Down approach with a difference that we are doing it purposely.

DYM-Drill down approach is going to help in different areas in personal life, as a leader, as a software developer and in project management. This is something, now we are going to use to develop other skills

CHAPTER 04

Difference Between Manager and Leader

"You manage things. You Lead People"

Prime Minister Narendra Modi stated that he views himself not as a 'Pradhan Mantri' (Prime Minister), but as a Pradhan Sewak (Prime Servant), subtly shifting the perception of how a leader should govern a country. This change in terminology reflects his approach to leadership as one of service rather than authority.

Kautilya, also known as Chanakya, was an ancient Indian scholar and adviser to Chandragupt Maurya, the founder of the Maurya Empire. He authored the Arthashastra, a formative text on statecraft and economics, which discusses the duties of a ruler in depth.

The Arthashastra states,

"प्रजासुखे सुखं राज्ञः प्रजानां च हिते हितम्। नात्मप्रियं प्रियं राज्ञः प्रजानां तु प्रियं प्रियम्॥ (अर्थशास्त्र 1/19),

which translates to "The Happiness of the king lies in the happiness of the people; the welfare of the king is in the welfare of the people. The king has no personal desires; what is dear to the people is dear to him." This encapsulates the concept that a ruler is fundamentally a public servant, compensated for his services to the people.

According to this philosophy, our leader's success should be measured by the success of his team rather than his personal achievements. Leaders are tasked with serving their team by motivating and training them to meet organizational goals. By emphasizing this aspect of leadership as a fundamental duty it can significantly enhance their effectiveness and commitment to their roles.

Instilling the belief that a leader's success is gauged by their team's achievements, transforms the mind frame of leaders, and leadership practices involved. They are compensated to serve their team by motivating and training them, doing whatever is necessary to achieve the team's organizational goals. Communicating these fundamental traits can significantly impact their effectiveness and approach to leadership.

नेतृत्व का उद्देश्य लोगों को सही रास्ता बताना है हुकूमत करना नहीं

The purpose of a leader is to guide people on the right path, not to overrule or govern them

The terms manager and leader often cause confusion but are fundamentally different, a fact that many people find intriguing. Throughout my journey I have explored these distinctions and would love to share these insights, which may open many eyes. In the views of a layman, the meaning of these two terms may not hold much of a difference, but the fact of the matter is that they are completely different from one another. The entire focus of my exploration has revolved around this differentiation, and I would love to take you all for a ride. It will prove to be an eye-opener for many.

First off, let's give ourselves a minute and reflect on the following questions.

What exactly separates a manager from a leader?

Are there simply two titles for the same role or do they represent distinct approaches to guiding others?

What are your thoughts on this?

Let's examine these roles more closely and understand why recognizing the difference is so important in the professional world.

Here are ate attributes of manager and leaders.

MANAGER	LEADER
Output oriented	People-Oriented
Delegates responsibilities	Delegates Authorities
Shows 'Who's Wrong'	Shows What's Wrong
Drives Team Members	Coaches Team Members
Presumes	Explores
Seeks Control	Seeks Commitment
Orders	Challenges
Creates Fear	Creates Confidence
Positional Power	Personal Power
Keeps Distance	Makes Contacts
Says What to Do	Shows How to Do
Demands Respect	Commands Respect
Works In the System	Works on the System
Gets Best Out of Resources	Organizes Best Resources
System-Centric	People-Centric
Professional (IQ)	Emotional (EQ)
Directional	Inspirational
Systematic	Charismatic

You will notice how the choice of words can significantly impact perception. Let me illustrate with a simple example. In the last chapter, we learned about deep diving, now let's explore in depth the difference between a housewife and a homemaker. Consider how people refer to a woman who doesn't work outside the home but takes care of her household. Some might call her a housewife, which can suddenly imply that she is merely fulfilling a duty. On the other hand, the term homemaker suggests that she's actively creating a nurturing environment positioning her as a valuable contributor. Upon deeper analysis, the term 'housewife' appeared to connote a liability, whereas 'homemaker' resonated as an asset.

Here's another example: Someone might be described as stubborn versus determined. While stubborn might carry a negative connotation of being unreasonable, determined conveys a positive sense of perseverance and dedication. Similarly describing someone as thrifty vs cheap changes the narrative: Thrifty suggests careful and prudent financial management, whereas cheap might imply a reluctance to spend money even when necessary.

By understanding the depth of words, when you feel these distinctions in your mind you'll transform into a different kind of leader. This method allows us to breakdown behaviours and rolls into smaller understandable parts making it clearer how much each contributes uniquely to an organization's success.

In addition, here are a couple of key distinctions explained in simple terms.

Leaders are People-Centric

Managers are output centric. They prioritize meeting deadlines, hitting targets and ensuring that every piece of work is completed on time. This approach is essential for maintaining productivity and ensuring operational success. In contrast, Leaders are people centric. Leaders focus on motivating, developing, and supporting team members. They believe that satisfied and well cared for employees will naturally lead to high productivity and better results. This people centric approach helps build a motivated and committed workforce

Leader's delegates authorities rather than just the responsibilities

Managers often delegate responsibilities to their team members. This means assigning tasks and expecting team members to follow through on specific instructions without much room for personal judgment or decision making. It's a structured way to ensure that specific jobs are completed as required. Leaders however delegate authority which involves empowering team members by giving them the power to make decisions within the certain boundaries. This empowerment encourages team members to take ownership of their work and foster a sense of responsibility and engagement. It helps build trust and encourages professional growth and autonomy among team members.

These examples show how managers and leaders apply different strategies to achieve success within an organization. Managers might focus more on the mechanics of task completion wild leaders emphasize the growth and well-being of their team members believing that a strong team naturally leads to the best outcomes. In continuation let us check out the behavioural patterns of leaders and its impact on their teams.

Leaders Coach Team Members

Unlike managers who drive team members to complete tasks leaders act more like coaches. They invest time in understanding each team member's strengths and weaknesses. Instead of driving what to do, they put open-ended questions "what will they do, how will they do it, what challenges they foresee and how can they overcome these challenges etc.". This coaching mentality helps develop skills within the team, Empowering individuals to take on new challenges and grow professionally.

Leaders Create Confidence instead of Fear

Leaders aim to build a supportive and encouraging environment. Instead of using their positions to instil fear for motivation they use personal power to foster trust and respect. This approach creates a workplace where team members feel secure and valued, which is conducive to innovation and creative problem solving. Leaders encourage open communication and feedback which supports a culture where employees are not afraid to express ideas or concerns.

In this chapter, I shared around 18 key differences between managers and leaders and have explained a few of them. I will leave the explanation of the other differences for you to explore on your own. With deep-dive skills and the knowledge of the differences I've shared, I am confident you can identify the other differences on your own.

The capacity of a leader to energise and motivate their colleagues is a fundamental quality. They are not just charming and methodical in their approach, which facilitates deeper connections with others.

Leaders share a compelling vision that helps align the team's efforts. They excite and motivate their team not just about the work at hand but about the bigger picture and how each role contributes to overall success.

By focusing on these leadership behaviours, we see a dynamic that extends beyond just managing tasks to truly leading people. Leaders Foster and environment where team members are motivated to not only meet but exceed expectations because they feel genuinely engaged and invested in their work. The distinction between managing and leading can thus be seen as the difference between ensuring tasks are completed and inspiring a team to achieve greatness.

I leave you to ponder further on how these differences might manifest in your own workplace or leadership style. How do you see the roles of manager and leader playing out in your professional experiences?

CHAPTER 05

The Winning Spirit and Power of Positive Thinking

"You are the leader of your own journey"

Every company environment has a significant and broad impact from leadership. Projects and tasks are guided by leaders, who also mould the emotional climate of the company. It is thus impossible to exaggerate the influence of optimistic thinking on leadership. It changes obstacles into chances and disappointments into teaching moments.

Consider, for instance, that a quarterly report reveals the company has not been able to achieve its objectives. Dev, mentioned in the initial chapters, reacts with blame or hopelessness, which only demoralizes the team and skews their judgment. The result is tense moods, inhibited communication, and stifled creativity.

Out of fear of being criticized or failing, employees may start to adopt Dev's mindset, becoming less willing to put in extra effort or suggest new solutions. They are afraid of being judged or failing.

On the other side, a leader who adapts to a constructive attitude towards the same situation can view the missed goals as an important indication of where the team still has to go in order to arrive at their desired destination.

It is possible that a leader of this kind would proclaim that this illustrates precisely where we need to concentrate our efforts. Using this as a guide, let us rethink our ideas and come back even stronger than before.

Here, the focus is not on failure but rather on the possibilities and opportunities for improvement. High morale is maintained through the implementation of this method, which also fosters a culture in which problems are confronted and handled openly rather than being feared. A significant number of knock-on effects are brought about by this constructive method. Team members who feel empowered and appreciated are more likely to focus their whole attention on their work at hand. They see problems as collective team concerns that need to be resolved rather than as individual barriers to be surmounted.

All team members have the chance to develop in an atmosphere that positive leaders create by seeing every day as a fresh chance to both inspire and be inspired. An upbeat attitude can turn into a self-fulfilling vision, which means that there is a higher chance that the team will succeed the more firmly a leader feels they can. As such, having a positive mentality is essential for both long-term success and general happiness in the corporate world.

When challenges or problems arise, overcoming them or transforming them into opportunities is fundamentally a mental process. The ability to perceive difficulties not as obstacles but as catalysts for growth reinforces the power of a positive outlook. This mental strategy not only propels themes towards success but also cultivates resilience and adaptability, essential qualities in any thriving corporate environment.

- **THE MIND GAME**

When you focus on problems, you will have more problems. But when you focus on possibilities, you will have more opportunities. It is a rather very simple game and as Dr.Wayne Dyer says, "What you think, you become". In order to be able to create something extraordinary for yourself or for people around you, all it takes is your "thoughts". Always think good, powerful, and positive things and the outcome will be so magical that you would be pleasantly surprised by its spell

"When Mind is weak, a situation becomes a Problem.
When Mind is balanced, the situation becomes a challenge
When Mind is strong, the situation becomes an Opportunity"

Opportunities come in all shapes, sizes, and shades of life. An otherwise seemingly normal incident may prove disastrous to someone or beneficial and a blessing to the other. It can turn into a beautiful proposition only if we know how and what to make of it. There is no dearth of opportunities for the one who has a progressive mindset because only that individual can turn stone into gold. The ability to find the diamond in the midst of millions of coal rests with that mind that can perceive and steer the darkness away into a ray of bright new sunshine.

- **POWER OF POSITIVE THINKING**

We can achieve something only if we believe in that. To attain a conscious and permanent state of perfect equilibrium, whether mental, psychological, emotional, physical, or moral we ought to understand the concept of "positive thinking."

दवा असर तभी करती है जब हम उस में विश्वास खोल देते हैं
"Medicine works only if you are positive about it"

When you further move ahead to meet your goals, you will find many hurdles, maybe multiple failures. Understand in all battles, whether someone wins or loses, both lose something and building this losing attribute into a positive makes you successful. you have to take calculated risks. So, to win any battle, you have to be ready to face the failure and keep moving. This can only happen if you are positive about your goal(s).

- **BE PASSIONATE ABOUT YOUR GOALS**

The consistency and determination depend on whether or not you will ever be able to live up to your expectations! And that is when the degree of your desire either creates or deteriorates the energy that will lead to its final outcome. The conviction and certainty in your thoughts, actions, and plan will make you or break you. Because at the end of the day, you ought to feel genuine respect and adulation in your own eyes first! If that happens, you are sure to make an impact on whosoever you relate it with. People will be able to identify themselves with your victory and maybe even learn from your wisdom.

Remember few rules for building consistency and determination:

1. **लड़ाई मर के नहीं मार के जीती जाती है** ***You can't win by killing yourself***

   You have to ensure that you kill all small / big hurdles you get on the way of your success. Killing yourself (depression etc) is not going to help you winning the game

2. **देश के लिए मरना आसान है, देश के लिए जीना सीखे** ***(Its more difficult to live rather than die for your country)***

   This quote inspires us that to achieve something, onetime sacrifice will not work, we must put in continuous efforts, and we need to live for the goal. Living for goal means killing yourself on a daily basis.

3. **लड़ने के लिए मारने की नहीं मार खाने की हिम्मत चाहिए**

   (To fight, you need courage rather than just the power)

   You may reach to a stage where you feel, there is no further path to meet your goal, all paths are closed. At this stage the following philosophy works the best.

4. **किसी को इतना मत डराओ कि डर खत्म हो जाए.**
जब डर लग रहा हो तो खुद को इतना डराओ कि डर खत्म हो जाए क्योंकि डर के आगे जीत है
(Ahead of fear, there is victory)

Understand, to achieve your goal, you have to be confidently positive that you can, and you will win it. This will motivate you to keep moving and remember the story of Rabbit & Tortoise, where tortoise wins the race because of being consistent.

We've recognized the significance of a positive mindset and a winning spirit, **yet it's essential to understand that without action – Karma - these positive intentions remain just that, intentions!!** This concept of action as a cornerstone of success, connects seamlessly with the visual interpretations provided by the images. Let's take a look and understand the entire theory/belief/notion, revolving around, 'action.'

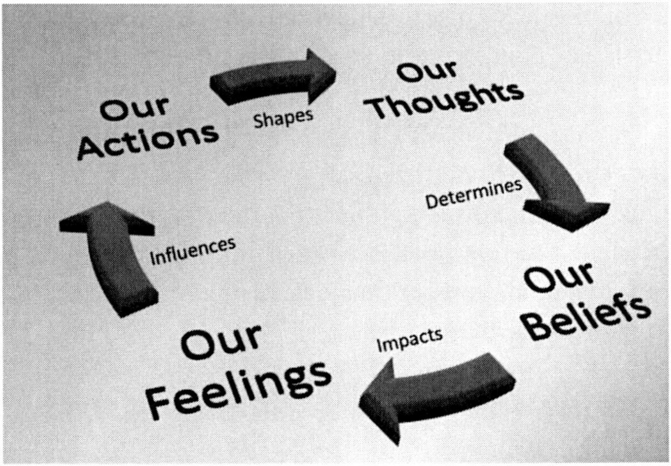

The image depicts a cyclical diagram illustrating the interconnection between our actions, feelings, thoughts, and beliefs. It shows that our actions influence our feelings which in turn shape our thoughts. These thoughts determine our beliefs, and our beliefs impact our actions, creating a continuous loop. This cycle emphasizes how each component is crucial in shaping our overall mindset and behaviour, suggesting that changes in any one area can affect the entire circle, potentially leading to personal development and growth.

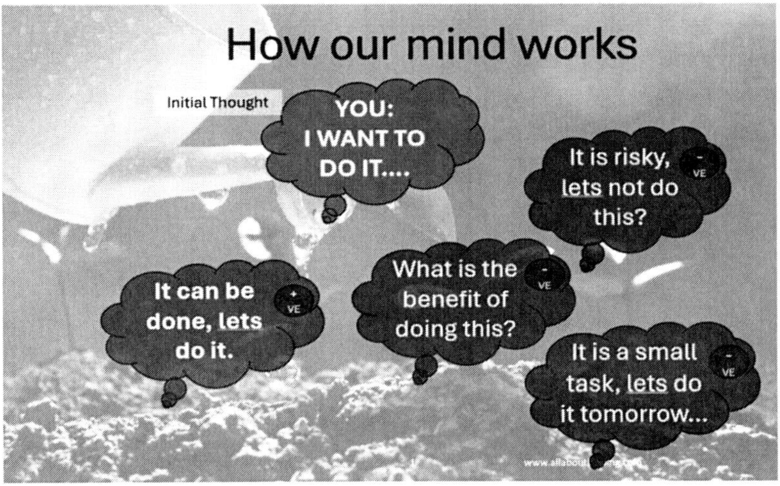

This illustration depicts the dynamic conversation happening in our mind when we face a decision. At the centre, there's a speech bubble (labelled as 'initial thought' that shows your initial enthusiasm, saying" I WANT TO DO IT...
"Surrounding this area are those other bubbles in +ve & --ve each representing different facets of our thinking process.

The bubbles (with -ve on top right) bring up concerns and delays. One suggests caution because of risk: "It is risky, let's not do this!" Another questions the utility: "What is the benefit of doing this?" There's also a hint of procrastination: "It's a small task, let's do it tomorrow..."

In contrast, the bubble (with +ve on top tight) brings optimism and action, saying, “It can be done, let’s do it.” This shows how our mind can motivate us, pushing through the doubts and fears from the blue bubbles.

Together, these bubbles (thoughts) capture the competing thoughts that can either empower or hinder us, highlighting the complexity of our decision-making process.

“Which thoughts should we nurture?”
Consider that everything I have achieved and will achieve stems from my actions and efforts. Therefore, it’s important for me to continue striving forward with humility and determination.

This message aligns with the famous verse from the Bhagavad Gita.
Sanskrit (Devanagari Script)
कर्मण्येवाधिकारस्ते मा फलेषु कदाचन।
मा कर्मफलहेतुर्भूर्मा ते संगोऽस्त्वकर्मणि॥

Transliteration (Hindi):
अर्थ: तेरा कर्म करने में ही अधिकार है, उसके फलों में कभी नहीं। इसलिए तू कर्म के फल हेतु मत हो तथा तेरी कर्म न करने में भी आसक्ति न हो।

English Translation:
You have a control on your actions, never on the result. So let the focus not be the result (fruit), and never be inactive.

This is a quote from the Bhagavad Gita, emphasizing the philosophy of doing one's duty without attachment to the results. To further understand and correctly comprehend the above-mentioned, let me put it in the simplest of words.

"Karm", action, is something that is in our control, but the 'phal', result is not in our control. So, all we need to do is keep the action going Without worrying about the outcome, ensuring we remain engaged and diligent in our efforts regardless of what the results might be.

I would like to add here: it is important to note that actions performed with integrity, sincerity, and a clear conscience are more likely to bear positive outcomes. While the results are not directly under our control, honest and ethical actions set a strong foundation for favourable results. Thus, maintaining a commitment to these principles in our actions can lead to beneficial consequences over time.

Adding a playful note many might not fully understand the law of attraction where the universe seems to bring you more of what you focus on. Well in today's world it seems Google has become that universe always ready to show you more of what you've been searching for, whether you asked for it again or not!

This reminds me about Thomas Friedman's book, "The World is Flat." The book draws attention to the early 2000s when many jobs shifted to India and China, effectively shrinking global distances. He illustrates how travel communication and shipping have become straightforward and inexpensive, making any job or service globally outsourceable, thus opening up both opportunities and challenges for nations and individuals.

Friedman elaborates that in such a flat world, changes occur rapidly. It is crucial to adapt our educational approaches to help our children thrive in this environment. Instead of perceiving global interconnectedness as a threat they should see it as a fertile ground for opportunities

He emphasizes the importance of teaching children to be lifelong learner's adept at acquiring new skills and knowledge. He sums this up in the formula as

CQ (Curiosity Quotient) + PQ (Passionate Quotient) > IQ (Intelligence Quotient)

Suggesting that in a world where information is ubiquitous, curiosity and passion can surpass traditional measures of intelligence like IQ in determining success.

For instance, consider how a child's simple curiosity about how plants grow can lead them to learn more about biology, agriculture, or even climate science. Their initial passion might lead them to participate in science fairs join environmental clubs or follow educational videos and articles online. This hands-on, interest-driven learning is more impact impactful and lasting compared to routine memorization.

Therefore, fostering curiosity and passion in learning is essential. These traits empower individuals to navigate and leverage the rapidly changing, flat world efficiently transforming potential challenges into opportunities for personal and professional growth.

Here are the key takeaways from this chapter:

1. Thinking positively and keeping an eye on the bigger picture can lead to better and bigger outcomes.
2. Staying positive helps maintain motivation, even after setbacks, encouraging continued effort.
3. Always aim to win. A winning mindset boosts positivity and motivation.
4. Action is necessary for results. A constructive outlook/viewpoint, thinking big, and a winning attitude motivate action.
5. Your achievements are the direct result of your actions, so, act towards your goals, consistently.

CHAPTER

06

The Dynamics of a Calm & Composed Mind

"Don't let people pull you into their storm.
Pull them into your peace"

Among the most important but sometimes disregarded elements of the path to good leadership is the relationship between mental health and leadership positions.

This asks a leader to be more in touch with their inner self and the people they lead than it does with a strong business plan. It can broaden our eyes to see how multifaceted both we and our team members are. Fundamentally, there are several tiers to our existence, and each one shapes our interactions with the outside world and our sense of our place there. Each layer—from the physical body to more profound components like the mind, intellect, and even the ego—is essential to determining our leadership effectiveness.

Physical sickness, like having a persistent headache, battling a cold or dealing with back pain, can dim our usual sharpness and slow our responsiveness, making it challenging to lead effectively.

Just as these physical elements impact our ability to engage fully, mental stress can also cloud our judgement. When our minds are occupied with worries or we feel overweight by stress, it becomes difficult to deliver what is expected from the audience or the team, which also disrupts our ability to listen attentively to our team and make thoughtful decisions. This mental clutter not only hampers leadership abilities but also affects the overall atmosphere of our team, making it a true shell for leaders to manage both their physical health and mental well-being.

As shared above, several tiers to our existence, shape our interactions with the outside world. Let me first share the concept of "The Seven Levels of Existence."

The concept of the Seven Levels of Existence provides a profound framework to explore the various layers that constitute our existence, from the physical to the spiritual. Each level offers unique insights into how we interact with the world and ourselves. As we explore these magical layers, we will gain a unique understanding of our actions, thoughts, emotions and the essence of our true selves. Here is a brief overview of these levels, highlighting their significance & interconnections.

Let us stretch from the tangible to the subtle (सूक्ष्म).

1. **Body:** At the most tangible level, our body is the physical aspect through which we interact with the world. It is the vessel that carries out actions and senses the environment around us
2. **Breath:** Breath is not only essential to life, but it also is the bridge between the body and the mind. Focusing on breath is a powerful tool for regulating our emotional state and energy levels.
3. **Mind:** this layer encompasses our thoughts, emotions and perceptions. The reason why we process information and experience greatly influences how we view the world and ourselves
4. **Intellect:** Beyond the reactive mind lies the intellect, the level of reasoning and understanding. This is where we analyse information, make decisions and discern between right and wrong.
5. **Memory:** Serving as a personal archive, memory holds past experiences and knowledge. It shapes our identity and influences our reactions and decisions based on previous learning.

6. **Ego:** At this level, we find our self-image how we perceive ourselves, and the opinions we hold about our capabilities and worth. While a healthy ego can build confidence, areas of unbalanced ego can skew our perceptions and interactions.
7. **Soul/Self/Consciousness:** The deepest and most subtle layer is our soul or consciousness. This is our true essence; beyond the physical or mental identities we carry. It connects us with a universal sense of being and provides an inner sense of peace and stability.

This holistic approach inspires us to embrace calmness and depth, enhancing our interactions and experiences. It promotes a balanced life, and nurturing a positive environment supports both personal and professional development. By prioritising our inner well-being, we strengthen our connections and leadership, contributing to a supportive and flourishing community.

The stress in our mind is not just about what we have in hand, but it is more because of overthinking or thoughts going in our minds. If you focus on thoughts, you will see they are either some bad experiences from the past or some worries of the future. Try to visualize the emotions you get when you think about any negative past thoughts, you will notice the emotions you have are anger, betrayal, frustration, etc. The instant impact on the body is, rise in the temperature. Whereas when we think about future worries, the body temperature, drops. The thoughts pendulum between past to future and vice versa keep changing the body temperature too and this pendulum scenario fluctuates our body temperature, kills our body energy and makes our mind restless.

"Yesterday is history, tomorrow is a mystery, and today is a gift--that is why it is called the present."

So, we all need to learn to be in present moment. But the more we try to depress the past or future thought, more they got active. So, the mantra to suppress them is to ignore them by telling your mind to give 100% to what you are doing in present moment.

Give 100% to what you are doing in present moment

Living in the 'current moment' is essential to good leadership. It means concentrating on the here and now, lessening outside distractions like fears about the future or failures in the past. Whether they are doing strategic planning or attending a crucial team meeting, leaders who have this focus are more effective. Leaders who use these techniques can better oversee their duties and their interactions with their team members. Any leader needs mental flexibility to accept and adjust to the realities of any circumstance without allowing prejudices or preconceptions to govern reactions. This not only keeps a perspective balanced but also creates a positive and encouraging work environment.

Before we move forward, I will share the four elements without which we wouldn't survive.
They are the four energy sources, Food, Breath, Sleep, and a Calm or Peaceful Mind. Sleep and food are limited resources, whereas breath and clam or peaceful mind are unlimited. Once puzzled, as you might be, I learned the power of breath when someone showed me how they fuel action. Let us take a simple example that all of you will be able to relate to. When you have to lift something very heavy, what is the first thing that you do? You inhale. That breath that you take in and hold enables you to complete your task.

I have shared the above with you as an example, but I have seen it in front of my eyes being demonstrated. At first, I did not realise what was going on, but when the theory behind it was explained, I was in awe. This energy source, called breath, contains a lot of energy. Every single breath that we take has the potential to move mountains.

The whole idea of emphasising this source of energy is that if we practice breathing exercises and watch our breath, our minds will be in a calm state. Individuals who have to lead must have a relaxed mind. A restful mind will perceive better, make clearer decisions, foster creativity, build stronger relationships, and inspire confidence in others.

Meditation, when connected to conscious breathing, gives you pure serenity (शांति), and the power of 'quiet' has been made understood. This also helps us align ourselves with different spheres of existence; from the physical to the emotional.

With my experience, I have come to realise that mindfulness, or mental health, is an unsurpassable attribute to becoming a good human being and a great leader. I firmly believe Breath is an unlimited source of energy.

TAKEAWAYS FROM THIS CHAPTER

1. Mental health and leadership: A calm and restful state of mind enables a leader to make clear decisions, nourish creativity, build stronger relationships, and inspire confidence in others.
2. The Seven Levels of Existence: This paradigm helps us to comprehend ourselves and our relationship to the outside world by providing insights into the levels of our being.
3. The four sources of energy: Focus on the need to know and use the four energy sources to improve clarity, vigour, and leadership.
4. Live in the 'current moment.': This develops awareness, lowers tension, sharpens concentration, and promotes closer relationships with oneself and other people.
5. To live in present, the tool is to give 100% to what you are doing in the current moment.
6. Meditation and breathing exercises are the tools to relax and calm your mind.

Leaders who live in the present with less disturbing thoughts help him in the following ways:

1. Cultivating clarity: improved focus and concentration lead to better decision-making.
2. Stress reduction: lower stress levels result in a calmer, more composed leadership presence.

3. Emotional regulation: enhanced self-awareness fosters better management of emotions, which is crucial for effective leadership.
4. Creativity boosts: clearing the mind through meditations parks creativity and innovative thinking.
5. Enhance resilience: regular practice builds mental resilience, enabling leaders to navigate challenges with composure.

CHAPTER 07

Emotional Intelligence (EI)

"It takes something more than Intelligence to act intelligently"

There have been a lot of noise about Emotional Intelligence (EI). EI first came into existence in the year 1990. Mayer and Salovey have been the first to have coined the term. Later in 1995, Emotional Intelligence won extensive popularity by American psychologist, Daniel Goleman. And his book, "Emotional Intelligence" Bantram 1995, won much-deserved acclaim and recognition.

We have leaders who have emotional intelligence are more likely to realize when pride and emotions are influencing their thinking, allowing them to make more rational, impartial choices. In addition to reigning in your own feelings, emotional intelligence makes it easier to anticipate and respond to others' sentiments.

When talking about a leader, we ought to understand that to build a happy, and consistent, result-oriented team, he/she will have to work on the practice of EI at a very significant level. It may seem tricky, but the sailing will get smooth if the empathy and concern factor remains intact at all times. We have leaders who have emotional intelligence are more likely to realize when pride and emotions are influencing their thinking, allowing them to make more rational, impartial choices. In addition to reigning in your own feelings, emotional intelligence makes it easier to anticipate and respond to others' sentiments.

EQ separates great performers in the workplace from the good ones. It affects how we manage behavior, navigate social complexities, and make personal decisions that achieve positive results. Therefore, people with strong emotional intelligence are

more likely to succeed than those with high IQs or relevant experience.
End number of studies have been carried out and numerous studies have been exhausted to understand EI.
But the one psychologist that I would like to speak about here is Daniel Goleman. He is an internationally known psychologist who lectures frequently to professional groups, business audiences, and on college campuses.

According to Goleman, EI is a cluster of skills and competencies, which are focused on four capabilities: **self-awareness, relationship management, and social awareness.** This American psychologist who helped to popularize emotional intelligence, says that there are five key elements of emotional intelligence:

1. Self-awareness.
2. Self-regulation.
3. Motivation.
4. Empathy.
5. Social skills.

The above-mentioned points are, in some way or the other, related. But let us first take them one by one.

Self-awareness is the ability to recognize and understand your moods, emotions and drives as well as their effects on others. It is all about knowing your personal strengths and weaknesses and having a strong sense of your own worth. We all have weaknesses in us, but they can be overcome if we are able to identify them in the first place. Self-awareness is the base to our second element; Self-Regulation.

Self-regulation speaks about managing emotions and think before acting.

Self-regulated people **can calm themselves down when they're angry or upset and** cheer themselves up when they're down. They are also flexible and adapt their styles to work with their colleagues (no matter who they are) and take charge of situations when necessary.
Whether a leader or a team member, it is imperative for every human being to be able to access their bouts of situational feelings, under tabs. If one is able to do that, more than half the battle is won.

Motivation is that feather you wear in your hat when your drive for life is on an all high. An individual who understands the importance of self-love can forever remain motivated. There should always be scope for self-improvement because that is what will aid you in constant growth in life. Life is a combination of the good and bad. Not everything happens the way we want it to. To be able to forge ahead with rejuvenated spirits is the true mark of a successful human being. Goleman's Motivation states as having an interest in learning and self-improvement. It is having the strength to keep going when there are obstacles in life. It is setting goals and following through with them.

Empathy is the ability to put yourself in the second person's shoes and take a feel of what she/he is going through. This will help you understand the other individual's feelings. It is also important to share the empathy.

In today's world, people have become very practical in life. They always want to find a logical and reasonable understanding of things, situations. They want a scientifically substantiated outlook on practically everything that surrounds them. We are all turning into machines. Simply working, meeting deadlines, and going crazy in this mad world, we forget the biggest yet simplest point, being empathetic!

For how long we will find true happiness in machines and gadgets. At the end of the day, we need someone who genuinely cares for us. And this care turns millionfold if we have the ability to love them back. To be able to understand the feelings of people around you, be it home, workplace, or a whole community. If you are cold enough to never be able to touch their hearts, you have essentially failed in life.

Goleman says Empathy is generally defined as the extent to **which one has the ability to understand and accept another's feelings and emotions.** He adds, empathy–one of the basic components of emotional intelligence–is a critical part of social awareness, and, as such, key to success in life.

Social skills are the **emotional intelligence skills to properly manage one's and others' emotions**, to connect, interact and work with others. If empathy is outward-driven to the others, social skills are inward-driven and focus on how to interact with and leverage others to reach our goals.

As I had mentioned earlier, EI encompasses a list of selected traits that are interdependent and interrelated. The absence of even one of them will yield temporary, and weak results. Even if they look positive, they will be short-lived. A mix of all the points enhances the growth of an individual. And it is apparently clear that we can grow, only if we can bring growth in others.

THE BENEFITS OF EI. Increasingly we are working in organizations with different cultures, genders, generations, geographical locations, work pressures. The following points will benefit you tremendously if you follow EI

- Think before you speak
- Develop meaningful long-lasting relationships

- Understand others
- Enable others to become more productive
- Improve your communication style
- Be proactive with situations that create conflict

How to work on Emotional Intelligence

Improving your emotional intelligence cannot be achieved through a single process or plan. Attending a workshop, reading a book, or undergoing training won't instantly enhance your EQ. This is because emotional intelligence is not a straightforward hard skill. Instead, it consists of various soft skills.

I like to think of emotional intelligence as a balance between the head and the heart. Have you ever felt torn between what your mind tells you and your heart desires?

When faced with a choice between what is right and what is kind, always choose kindness, as it is inherently right.

This idea suggests that intellect (Mind) and kindness (Heart) often offer different perspectives. Finding a balance between thinking logically and feeling empathetically is essential for building emotional intelligence.

In the upcoming chapters. We will explorer different techniques to develop and strengthen your emotional quotient.

Keep reading...

EQ sets great performers apart from good ones in the workplace. It influences how we manage behavior, navigate social complexities, and make decisions that lead to positive outcomes. Therefore, people with strong emotional intelligence are more likely to succeed than those with just high IQs or relevant experience.

IQ tests evaluate your ability to solve problems, use logic, and understand or communicate complex ideas. In contrast, EQ tests assess your ability to recognize emotions in yourself and others and to use that awareness to guide your decisions.

The five key elements of emotional intelligence are:

1. Self-awareness
2. Self-regulation
3. Motivation
4. Empathy
5. Social skills

While a high IQ can help you succeed academically, a high EQ is essential for success in life. IQ involves making decisions with your mind, whereas EQ involves making decisions with your heart.

CHAPTER 08

Be Non-Judgmental

"Be someone who judges no one"

Let us get into another very interesting human trait, i.e., being non-judgemental.

How many of us understand the meaning of being non-judgemental?

There is a very famous saying, 'Do not judge a book by its cover.'

Being non-judgmental means seeing people and situations just as they are, without letting our opinions or preconceptions influence our view. It's about understanding that everyone has their own reasons and ways of doing things, which may be different from our own but are not necessarily wrong or inferior. This approach allows us to be more accepting and open to learning from the differences we encounter in others.

Try to understand that individuals who do not make impulsive judgements about others based on just what they observe are non-judgemental.

Consider the case of a team member who has been late for work for three days in a row. It's preferable to approach the circumstances knowing the facts, rather than jumping to the conclusion that this individual is always late. We may discover they are coping with health problems, family obligations, or inconsistent transportation by asking about their delay. With the use of this information, we can understand the bigger picture and react more effectively–for example, by giving them flexibility or assistance in solving problems.

In another situation, say, for instance, a female employee who always wears makeup and is well-dressed. Now, one day, she does not put on makeup but is dressed in her usual stylish attire. The first probable remark or thought that will come from her colleagues is, 'Why are you sad today? Is everything alright? They are just expressing themselves at a mere glance. It could be as simple as the fact that she did not feel like doing makeup, or, possibly, did not have the time as she was running late!

In another case scenario in the corporate world, picture a worker who routinely turns down chances to give a presentation at team gatherings or avoids taking on other challenges. Someone may need to pay attention to other aspects if they assume someone is not motivated or disinterested in their work. Through a nonjudgmental approach and conversation with the staff member, a manager may discover that the staff member experiences anxiety while speaking in front of an audience or feels unqualified for certain jobs. Recognising this, the manager could assist in training in communication or progressively expose the worker to these positions in a low-pressure, encouraging manner. This method helps to provide focused support that might improve the employee's capabilities and comfort level and clarify the reasons behind their behaviour. The outcome could be an increased sense of worth and appreciation for the worker, which would boost engagement and output at the workplace.

We open the door to greater understanding and productive communication when we decide not to pass judgement on someone right away. This method facilitates the creation of a supportive environment at work, in the classroom, or any other setting. It also makes it simpler to resolve conflicts in a positive way. So, the crux of the above examples narrows down to one aspect, i.e., do not make judgements based on partial or incomplete information.

There are two main **benefits of being non-judgmental.**
First, it allows you to be unbiased and open to understanding the facts of what happened.
Second, making judgmental statements can hurt the other person, leading them to respond similarly, which diverts the communication in a different direction.

In our daily interactions, understanding the difference between observation and judgement is crucial. An observation involves stating facts without attaching any personal views.

Let us take a few more simple case scenarios to understand the concept.

There are different ways we convert our observations into judgmental statements.

For instance, noting that the weather is sunny is an observation. On the other hand, calling the weather good adds a subjective opinion to the observation, reflecting a personal preference for sunshine, so it is a judgemental statement.

This is the first type of judgement, where we add a personal preference to the observation

Another example in a professional context, identifying that a report is missing two items is factual feedback. Critiquing the report as not good enough because of this omission is a judgement that can be perceived as criticism of the overall work rather than an objective assessment of its completeness.

This is the second type of being judgemental, where we generalise our observation.

Another example is when Person A is speaking loudly with person B, and you take this observation that Person A is angry, because, in general, our experience is that people's voices are raised when they are angry or agitated. Based on this, we conclude, that Person A is angry.

There is another type of being judgmental, where observation overlaps with our past experiences.

In one of the above examples, where an employee was reluctant to give a presentation in public, we assumed that he was not willing to work.

This is another way of being judgmental, where we assume, and give a verdict.

Making a judgemental statement here means we are all judgmental at some stage. Whether we generalise our observation, give a frame with some assumption, or use experience, etc.

It is very common that if I make some mistake, I will say, “I'm sorry, it was my fault.” But if the same is done by someone else, we begin to find the intention behind it!
Not binding the assumed intention with another's mistake is non-judgemental.

Emotionally, expressing that one feels sad is an acknowledgement of one's state of mind. Judging that feeling by saying one should not feel sad imposes a belief about the appropriateness of emotions, suggesting there is a right or wrong way to feel.

The distinction is vital because judgements can often be limiting and dismissive, while observations leave room for dialogue and understanding. Recognising this difference can help leaders and individuals create more supportive, inclusive, and communicative environments. It also encourages a mindset that is more accepting and less prone to snap judgements, leading to deeper connections and more effective problem-solving.

By understanding the above examples, it will be very clear and relatable to all you readers. This attribute of being 'non-judgemental', or, as I put it, 'it,' is **self-regulation,'** which is like a solid foundation for a leader.

But before we jump into more details, the one thing that needs to be understood is that leaders must take decisions (judgements). It is imperative to take some time to observe, evaluate, and then take a decision (judgement). Any decision which is purely based on observations/facts of all stakeholders with being empathetic, and no pre-biasing, and that is when you are truly called a 'non-judgemental' individual.

Understand, **to take right Judgments(decision), you should be non-judgemental.**

Embracing a non-judgmental approach as a leader brings numerous benefits, enhancing both personal effectiveness and team dynamics. Leaders who practice non-judgement foster an atmosphere of trust and openness. This openness encourages team members to share ideas and challenges without fear of harsh criticism, leading to innovative solutions and better problem-solving. When leaders hold off on immediate judgements, they gather more comprehensive information, which improves decision-making accuracy. This careful consideration ensures that decisions are well-informed and fair, boosting morale and respect among team members.

Leaders who are non-judgmental also contribute to a culture of learning and development. By understanding and addressing the unique needs and potential barriers faced by individuals, leaders can tailor support and development opportunities effectively. This personalised approach not only enhances individual performance but also aids in retaining talent, as employees feel valued and understood.

Let me explain another aspect of being non-judgemental, why people face challenges.

There are two types of challenges; Technical and Adaptive

Technical and adaptive challenges are distinct types of hurdles we encounter. Technical challenges are knowledge-based with defined solutions, while adaptive challenges are experience-based and require innovative approaches.

For example, if an individual is unable to use a new machine or a tool, he or she is facing a 'technical challenge.'

On the other hand, there is the adaptive challenge. Individuals who fall into this category have behavioural issues. This means they do not want to exit their comfort zones; hence, aligning with a new situation/role becomes an adaptive challenge.

Here is a breakdown of the key differences:

Technical Challenges

Technical challenges are well-defined problems with clear solutions. They are easy for everyone to identify and agree upon because they are rooted in science and technology. Solving them requires knowledge-based expertise in a particular process or system. Technical managers excel at addressing these challenges by utilizing their knowledge to implement solutions that people are generally receptive to.

Adaptive Challenges

Adaptive challenges are complex and often difficult to define. Unlike technical challenges, there is no single, universally agreed-upon root cause. They are based on human aspects like emotions and values, which can lead to differing perspectives. Because of this complexity, there are no one-size-fits-all solutions. Adaptive challenges require an experience-based approach that involves experimentation, learning, and potentially adapting mindsets. This is where emotionally intelligent leaders play a crucial role. They can guide people through the process of navigating these challenges, which can sometimes be met with resistance due to the need for change.

Under technical challenges, the competencies include:

- **Training System:** Establishing and using a structured program to enhance skills and knowledge.
- **Data Collection & Analysis:** Gathering information methodically and examining it to make informed decisions.
- **KRAs, SOPs, and Building Systems/Processes:** Defining key result areas and standard operating procedures to create efficient workflows.
- **Authority:** Using one's position to direct and control outcomes.
- **IQ:** Applying intellectual abilities to solve problems and make decisions.
- **Execution as Ability (Reviews):** The capability to carry out plans effectively and assess them regularly.
- **Resource Allocation & Optimisation:** Distributing and utilising resources most effectively.

For adaptive challenges, the competencies are:

- **Active Listening:** Fully concentrating on what is being said, understanding the message, and responding thoughtfully.
- **Ask Questions:** Inquiring to gain deeper insight and encourage exploration of ideas.
- **Acknowledgement of Diversity, Openness (Non-Judgmental):** Recognizing and valuing different backgrounds and perspectives and keeping an open mind.
- **Conversation:** Engaging in meaningful exchanges of ideas to foster understanding.
- **EQ:** Leveraging emotional intelligence to guide interpersonal relationships judiciously and empathetically.
- **Self-Awareness, Self-Regulation:** Understanding one's own emotions and impulses and managing them effectively.
- **Change/Adaptive/Flexible, Approachable:** Being able to adjust strategies as needed, being open to new ideas, and being easy to approach with concerns or new ideas.

In a nutshell, technical challenges are clear-cut solutions like a manual, flexible by experts, while adaptive challenges do not have perfect answers or solutions and require us to think, get on our feet, and break habits.

The reason I brought up these challenges is to highlight that there is no single right or wrong answer in adaptive challenges. Understanding this is key to being non-judgemental. Often, leaders might say something is not right based on their own perspective, but the other side could also have valid points.

"Something that is not right does not mean it is wrong. It is a key to be non-judgmental" **-Rajesh Sachdev**

Being non-judgmental means seeing people and situations just as they are, without letting our opinions or preconceptions influence our view.

It's about understanding that everyone has their own reasons and ways of doing things, which may be different from our own but are not necessarily wrong or inferior.

This approach allows us to be more accepting and open to learning from the differences we encounter in others.

Common mistakes, and how we make judgmental statements are

1) Labelling says a few instances or where we generalise our observation: "You always come late"
2) We add a personal preference to the observation. "The weather is good"
3) where observation overlaps with our past experiences. E.g. "Someone was loud, and we made the statement that he is angry.
4) We try to find the intention in another person's mistake

There are two main benefits of being non-judgmental.

First, you are not pre-biased and are open to understanding the facts of what happened. Second, when you make any judgmental statement, it hurts the second person, and second person starts defending the same and communication is diverted in a different direction.

There are 2 types of challenges – Technical & Adaptive. Adaptive challenges are related to people and are the main challenges leaders need to work on

Adaptive challenge has no right/wrong and accepting this is key to being non-judgmental and being empathetic

CHAPTER 09

Understand Your Emotions

"Your emotions are slaves of your thoughts
And you are slave of your emotions"

Have you ever felt that you were unable to express your emotions?

Or has it ever happened that your emotion was not understood by someone?

Have you once, if not often, pondered that someone could disregard your emotion/emotions, leaving you hurt and confused?

The answer to the above questions will undoubtedly be "YES."

This chapter will unfold layers of characteristics that you would probably never have comprehended about this seemingly very simple word, called '**emotion.**'

At one of my training workshops when I asked the participants to share one of their experiences when they were upset, what was it that they felt?

One of them shared that he has a colleague who constantly had his lunch at the workstation. To express what he felt at this instance, he replied," I felt that it is inappropriate to have lunch at the workstation." That is when I pointed out that this was his opinion and not his emotion. He then went on to say, "I felt that when one person can break the policy and eat at the workstation, this may encourage the other team members to follow the same."

I explained to him that this was still an opinion!

And then he expressed some frustration instead of sharing the feeling. That is when I explained that this attitude, or set of words, expressed an opinion, not a feeling.

In this case scenario the individual, undoubtedly, had a strong feeling, but he wasn't able to become aware of that feeling.

Now I stepped up and shared with the audience that it was not just the expression of a feeling but, there was a gap in identifying it, too! This is a very common aspect that people feel challenged when it comes to identifying and expressing their feelings. And it is more common among people in professions like lawyers, engineers, police officers, corporate managers, and career military personnel. That is because these sets of individuals use the left brain rather than the right one.

Now just put yourself in a similar situation, and think to yourself, "Am I able to identify my feelings or not?"

Ok, if I say, that you face challenges in expressing your emotions and feelings, you will probably disagree despite reading the earlier-mentioned examples.

I know by now how anxiously you would be waiting for the big reveal, so read on!

There are 3 levels of problems/mistakes we make when we express our feelings or thoughts.

The first and foremost we share our thoughts instead of feelings. In the above example, it will be interesting for you to know that there is an entire concept revolving around Feelings vs Thoughts. There are various challenges we face in expressing our emotions and feelings and we need to get to the bottom of this.

The second challenge

We do not have the right set of words for the expression of thoughts and feelings. And that is exactly where the problems or misconceptions begin.

Let's take an example to understand the second point better.

A good friend wanted to quit his job for the simple reason that he was annoyed with his reporting manager. When I repeatedly asked him, he said that the boss is full of arrogance and flares up on the smallest of matters. He gets provoked and seems angry at all times. It is getting very difficult to work under him. Also, a good relationship that we once shared, is all going down the drain.

I asked him to just relax a bit, and re-think with a calm mind and I asked him to refer to the 'list of feelings. I said to him that once you understand the list, just reconsider the actions and behaviour of your manager. Since he trusted me, he agreed to find out what was the magic behind the 'list of feelings' that could change my decision!

And bingo! When he understood the correct usage of words, he realised that in some cases, the manager was perhaps just impatient or annoyed. It helped him what was he missing, and soon enough, his insight completely transformed.

By using the list as a tool, he was able to understand his boss's hidden emotions. This helped him immensely in predicting the hidden cause behind the boss's seemingly irrelevant outbursts.

As a result, my friend continued working in the same company and with the same boss.

Having a simple understanding of the vocabulary that we use, can greatly enhance our ability to recognise and articulate our emotions. when you can precisely express how you feel, you can also better understand and manage those feelings. This improved intelligence allows you to differentiate between subtle nuances of emotions, enabling you to comprehend their origins, navigate them more effectively, and even reverse negative emotional states. Ultimately, the **"list of feelings"** empowers you to express yourself authentically and connect more deeply with others.

It is imperative to understand and follow the complete 'list of feelings and my reason behind saying so will be clear after the following example. Mr JK (protagonist) had a conflict of thoughts that occurred with a colleague turned friend who was assisting him in a project. Jk was very angry and full of rage, as perceived by her.

Now this is what we miss. When JK tried to understand what the reason behind his anger was. That was the time he followed the 'list of feelings' consciously. He then realized that the actual emotions were disappointment, irritation, and worry, while anger was only the outcome of these hidden emotions. Therefore, while identifying and expressing your feelings, make sure that the correct combination of words is used. The 'list of feelings' will make a significant difference in every area of your life. An additional aspect of this list is that you can rate the intensity of a word/words in each situation.

For your reference, I am sharing a table that contains the **'list of feelings'**

Feelings when your needs are satisfied

AFFECTIONATE	**CONFIDENT**	**GRATEFUL**	**PEACEFUL**
Compassionate	Empowered	Appreciative	Calm
Friendly	Open	Moved	Clear-headed
Loving	Proud	Thankful	Comfortable
Open Hearted	Safe	Touched	Centred
Sympathetic	Secure	**INSPIRED**	Content
Tender Warm	**EXCITED**	Amazed	Fulfilled
ENGAGED	Amazed	Awed	Mellow
Absorbed	Animated	Wonder	Quiet
Alert	Ardent	Joyful	Relaxed
Curious	Aroused	Amused	Relieved
Engrossed	Astonished	Delighted	Satisfied
Enchanted	Dazzled	Glad	Still
Entranced	Eager	Happy	Trusting
Fascinated	Energetic	Pleased	**REFRESHED**
Interested	Enthusiastic	Tickled	Enlivened
Intrigued	Giddy	**EXHILARATED**	Rejuvenated
Involved	Lively	Blissful	Renewed
Spellbound	Passionate	Ecstatic	Rested
Stimulated	Surprised	Elated	Restored
HOPEFUL	Vibrant	Radiant	Revived
Expectant		Thrilled	
encouraged			
optimistic			

Feelings when your needs are **NOT** satisfied

AFRAID	**PAIN**	**CONFUSED**	**AVERSION**
Apprehensive	Agony	Ambivalent	Animosity
Frightened	Anguished	Baffled	Appalled
Mistrustful	Bereaved	Bewildered	Contempt
Panicked	Grief	Dazed	Disgusted
Petrified	Heartbroken	Hesitant	Dislike
Scared	Hurt	Lost	Hate
Suspicious	Lonely	Mystified	Horrified
Terrified	Miserable	Perplexed	Hostile
Worried	Regretful	Puzzled	Repulsed

ANNOYED	ANGRY	EMBARRASSED	VULNERABLE
Aggravated	Enraged	Ashamed	Fragile
Dismayed	Furious	Chagrined	Guarded
Disgruntled	Incensed	Flustered	Helpless
Displeased	Indignant	Guilty	Insecure
Frustrated	Irate	Mortified	Reserved
Impatient	Outraged	Self-conscious	Sensitive
Irritated	Resentful		Shaky

One of the common mistakes we make by using words like Ignored/Threatened as a feeling. Words like "ignored" express how we interpret others, rather than how we feel. Here is a sampling of a few such words.

Abandoned	Misunderstood	Threatened
Abused	Neglected	Not appreciated
Betrayed	Provoked	Unheard,
Cornered	Taken for granted	Unseen
Manipulated		

For instance, if someone says, "I felt used because she/he has misused my reference". Normally people assume that by using the word "I feel", they are expressing their feelings. The words shared above are not actual feelings but opinions.

The Third Challenge

Even when we are identifying and expressing the right emotions, we still make another mistake, i.e., holding the other person responsible for our emotions. It is important to realise that we are responsible for our emotions. When we say, "You make me feel guilty," we're implying that someone else is in control of our feelings which isn't true. Our emotions are often tied to our needs. So, when expressing how we feel, instead of blaming someone else, we should focus on identifying and expressing our needs. By doing this, we take ownership of our emotions and can communicate more effectively with others.

Some simplified examples are as below:

1. **Disappointment** - The speaker feels disappointed because he was expecting one task to be completed but a team member didn't follow through.
2. **Sadness** - The speaker feels sad when an urgent client meeting comes up because he was hoping to spend time with family.
3. **Frustration** - The speaker feels frustrated when someone is late, and an important task is in the pipeline.

This shows that communication is important in any situation, be it work or personal life. By understanding how your words and actions can be interpreted by others, you can avoid causing frustration, anger, disappointment or sadness.

Using the same concept, a leader can rephrase thoughts from the second person into her/his need which can significantly change the perspective and approach to a scenario. It helps them focus on their feelings and needs rather than attributing their thoughts to intentions.

For example, if someone says, *"You never understood me".* Now you can interpret this line that her/his need to be understood is not fulfilled and take appropriate action.

By expressing our feelings in this way, we take ownership of our emotions and communicate more effectively with others.

THE MAIN PURPOSE OF THIS CHAPTER: MAKE YOU UNDERSTAND **YOUR** EMOTIONS IN THE RIGHT MANNER

Let's talk about different emotion moulds. Let me first explain what these moulds are. How are they created, and why do they exist?

Emotional moulds are the patterns and ways in which individuals perceive, experience, and express emotions. They are built over time through a combination of environmental factors, such as upbringing, family dynamics, societal influences, and personal experiences. These moulds are constructed through repeated interactions and responses to emotions within the environment. The formation of emotional moulds is also influenced by cultural norms, gender expectations, and societal stereotypes. These factors can shape how individuals learn to perceive and manage their emotions, leading to unique patterns of emotional expression and regulation. Overall, emotional moulds are the result of complex interactions between genetics, environment, and personal experiences. They play a significant role in shaping how individuals understand and navigate their emotional lives.

Let me now share some of the most common emotional moulds for a better interpretation.

- **Emotions are often seen as a sign of weakness**, but this belief is only a myth. As per my understanding, an individual who has the audacity or courage to show their emotions, are way stronger than the ones who don't. An emotionally expressive individual showcases her/his high EQ.
- **The idea that; boys don't cry;** is harmful and keeps outdated notions alive. A boy who falls and hurts himself might feel like he can't cry because he's supposed to be tough. But letting him cry and express his pain shows that it's okay to have feelings, no matter what the gender may be.
- The notion that **people will take advantage of you if you are soft** is a fear-based belief that does not always hold true. If

you are soft, people may be more supportive of you. There may be cases when people might take advantage, or they may not take soft-spoken people seriously. In such cases, if the leader shares the feedback, he/she will be able to manage it easily and effectively.

- **One must be rational and not emotional:** When any leader is too rational and believes only in right/wrong, people consider such a person as not flexible. They feel that he/she does not understand the other person situations (less empathetic). So, a leader should be, both, emotional and empathetic to be in a win-win situation.
- **Not showing emotions is a sign of maturity and strength:** Many believe that hiding emotions shows maturity and strength. However, showing emotions at the right time demonstrate strength and authenticity.
- **Anger, sadness, hurt, jealousy, and fear are all bad emotions** - All negative emotions allow identifying the unmet need: These emotions are often seen as bad, but they help identify what needs are not being met. For example, feeling jealous might show a need for recognition.
- **Compassion is very important in relationships**-maintain balance: Compassion is crucial for building strong relationships. Leaders should show understanding and care while also maintaining professional boundaries.
- **Unless you express anger and put pressure, people will not perform:** Some think that showing anger and putting pressure is necessary for performance. However, motivating through positive reinforcement and clear communication is often more effective. Pushing people with anger/pressure can have a negative impact on the motivation.

Now reflect on where we started this chapter from. You might be wondering why we're discussing emotions so extensively when they might seem straightforward. It's not easy; even after going through this chapter, you might still find it challenging. It's important to realize that expressing emotions appropriately requires consciousness and the right vocabulary.

Leaders, in particular, benefit from learning to express emotions correctly. They undergo self-transformation, can provide proper guidance to others, and develop a better understanding of others' emotions. Emotions are not easy to express; it's crucial to differentiate between thoughts and feelings, use the right vocabulary, and take ownership of your emotions as beneath your emotion lies your need.

You should consider using a "list of feelings" to help you to identify and express your emotions effectively and understand the underlying needs.

WHAT WE SAY	WHAT WE THINK	WHAT WE FEEL	ACCURATE STATEMENT
I feel betrayed.	I've been betrayed.	I feel sad, mad, and hurt.	I feel sad because I think I've been betrayed.
I feel stupid.	I think I am stupid.	I feel sad, ashamed and hurt.	I feel ashamed because I think I am stupid.
I feel broken.	I think I am broken.	I feel a painful sadness.	I think I am broken because I see myself as abandoned by other and feel a painful sadness.

CHAPTER 10

Understand and Control Your Behavior /Emotions

"Why We Do What We Do"

Ever heard the saying, "People can't change their basic behaviour"? Well, it turns out that might not be entirely true. But what if we know what drives our behaviour, can we change it now?

Imagine behaviour as an Iceberg, with only a small part visible above the water. That visible part is what we see on the surface, like someone's actions or reactions. But beneath the surface lies a whole world of factors that influence behaviour—things like beliefs, past experiences, emotions, and social norms. These hidden parts are like the roots of a tree, shaping and sustaining what we see above the surface.

So, when we want to change behaviour, we can't just focus on what's visible. We need to dive deep into the underlying factors, to understand why people act the way they do. By doing this, we can unlock the potential for real and lasting change.

Therefore, changing behaviour is about more than just what we see; it's about understanding the whole picture beneath the surface.

In this chapter we will understand a very effective tool or concept, that can assist us in understanding and changing our behaviour - it's called the **'Iceberg Model.'**

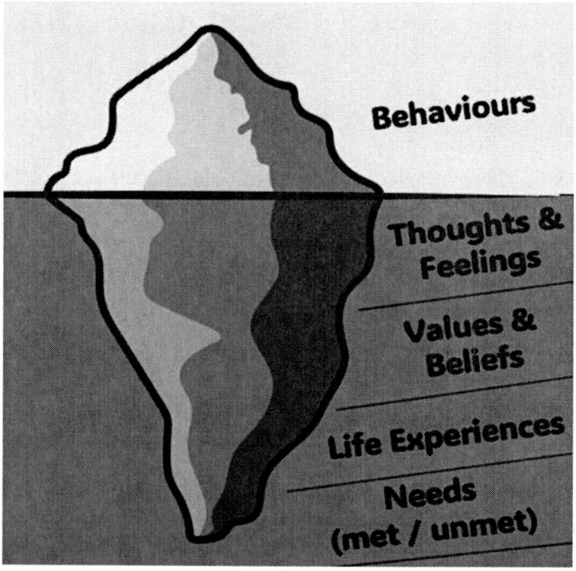

The Iceberg of You: Why We Do What We Do
Imagine you see someone shouting on the street. That's like the tip of an iceberg - you only see a small part of the story. There's a whole lot more going on underneath, just like with our actions!

The Iceberg Model explains why people act the way they do. It's like a giant iceberg floating in the ocean.

The Tip You See: This is the top of the iceberg, sticking out of the water. It's our actions and words that everyone can see. Like the yelling person on the street.

- **Behaviours:** The iceberg analogy helps us understand the hidden influences behind a person's approach to learning. The tip of the iceberg, visible above the water, represents the behaviours we can directly observe. This includes how they participate in class (asking questions, taking notes), how they complete assignments (carefully or rushed), and how they handle challenges (give up easily or persist). These actions are just the first glimpse into the deeper factors that influence learning.

The Hidden Story: This is the big part of the ice, hiding under the water. These are the things that influence how we behave, but we can't always see them right away. Here are some examples:

- **Thoughts and Feelings:** Ideas and emotions are like the surface of the ocean, just beneath the waves. Ideas are our thoughts - what we think and believe about ourselves and the world. Emotions, on the other hand, are the currents and experiences of feelings, such as joy, sadness, anger, or fear. In the previous chapter, we talked extensively about emotions and how they differ from the constant chatter of thoughts in our minds. If you haven't read that chapter yet, it's important to do so before continuing with this one.

- **Beliefs & Values:** What's important to us? For example, if someone believes everyone should be treated fairly, they might get upset if they see someone being bullied. These are the things that are important to a person. They influence how a person approaches learning and what they are motivated to learn. Another example is, that a person who values creativity may be more interested in open-ended learning tasks.

  Beliefs are like equations. Here are some of mine for reference:

  1. Work=Worship: I believe that dedicating ourselves to our work with passion and purpose is a form of worship, honouring our abilities and contributing to something greater.

2. Faster=Better: Efficiency and speed are crucial in achieving optimal results and progress in various aspects of personal and professional life.
3. Transparency=Trust: Being open and honest guilds trust, which forms the foundation of strong and meaningful relationships, leading to better outcomes.

- **Life Experiences:** This is that fine line that determines an individual's actions and reactions. Whatever we have experienced in the past, good and bad, undoubtedly impacts our present lives. We certainly cannot recall all of that we have experienced, and we cannot change that either. That is why it shows how we act in a certain manner in a given situation.
- **Needs Met/Unmet or Fears:** Every emotion we experience is rooted in either a met or unmet need, or a fear. Understanding these underlying factors can help us navigate our emotions more effectively.

At the end of this chapter, I'll provide a list detailing various needs and values to assist you in identifying your own.

How is this Iceberg Model helpful?

The iceberg analogy helps us understand the beliefs behind a particular behaviour of Self & Others too. By drawing the iceberg, we can uncover blind spots. Once we identify these beliefs that aren't helping us, we can work on changing them.

To explain the usage of an iceberg model, I am sharing a sample iceberg. The steps given below must be followed while you are creating your own.

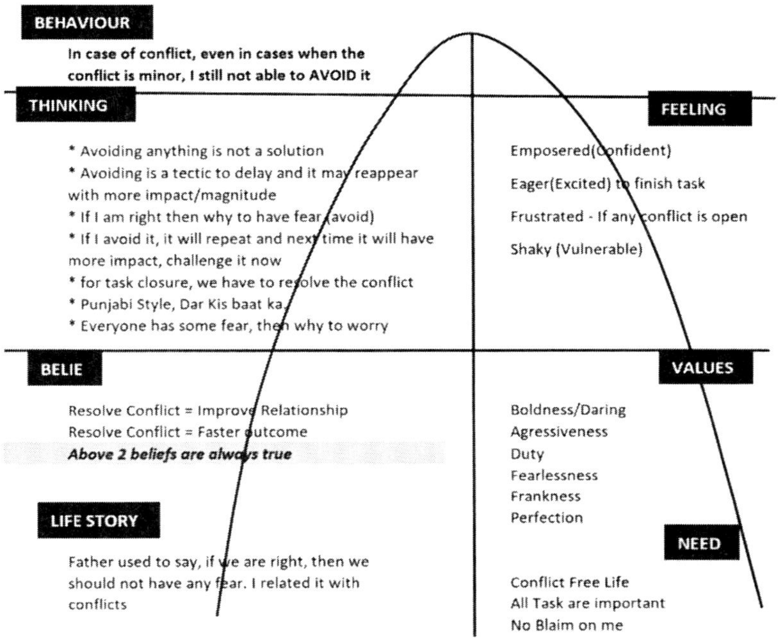

1. **Choose one Instance:** Focus on a single instance of the behaviour you want to analyse.
2. **Recall the Moment:** Take yourself back to that moment in the past to fully recall the instance.
3. **Reflect on Details:** Think about your behaviour, thoughts, feelings, and other relevant details. Write everything down. If needed. Close your eyes to immerse yourself fully in the memory.
4. **Stay Focused:** Do not mix different instances of the same behaviour, as each situation will have unique thoughts and feelings. Stick to one incident while analysing deeply.
5. **Use Available Resources:** Refer to lists of emotions, values and needs as necessary.
6. **Focus on Thoughts:** Pay particular attention to your thoughts and analyse what was going on in your mind (Thoughts). Pen them down, as each thought will give you

some input for any of the components needed in the iceberg.

7. **Avoid Self-Judgement:** While working on the iceberg, observe and write down exactly what you experienced without judging yourself.
8. **Belief Analysis:** Once you have a crystal-clear understanding of a few beliefs, you can determine which ones have been beneficial or detrimental to you.

We can dive in of what was the reason behind the other person's behaviour, we can understand him better and be more empathetic and can deal with the situation in a different and better way

How to dissolve the iceberg?

Once you have identified the belief behind a particular behaviour that is not helping you to meet your needs/values or you have uncovered a blind spot, you may have a question, can we dissolve the belief or remove the blind spot?

The good news is, that you can smash those roadblocks or your limited beliefs! Here's how:

1. **Identify Your Limiting Beliefs**
   Begin by pinpointing the beliefs that hold you back. If you're unsure where to start, focus on the most significant one first and then work through the others, one by one.
2. **Acknowledge It's Just a Belief**
   Understand that your belief is just that—a belief, not a fact. Challenge it by asking questions that broaden your perspective.
3. **Question Your Belief**
   Dive deeper into your belief by questioning its foundation, looking for supporting facts, and considering counteracting

evidence. Try to view it from different perspectives, such as someone successful or knowledgeable in the field.

4. **Recognize the Impact**
   Understand the negative impact your limiting belief can have. For example, believing you can't succeed because of a past failure may prevent you from seizing future opportunities.
5. **Adopt a New Perspective**
   Choose a new, empowering belief. While it may be challenging to change long-held beliefs, it's possible with courage and determination. Adopt a belief that aligns with your goals and supports your well-being.
6. **Put Your New Belief into Action**
   Take small steps that align with your new belief. For instance, if you thought you were too old to start exercising, begin with a short walk today. This not only reinforces your new belief but also helps establish a positive habit.

Overcoming limiting beliefs requires patience and persistence, but it can lead to a more fulfilling life.

In conclusion, the Iceberg Model is a helpful tool for understanding human behaviour. It shows that what we see on the surface is just a small part of a much larger picture. By looking beneath the surface, we can better understand why people act the way they do. This understanding can improve our communication, reduce misunderstandings, and help us develop empathy and compassion. By applying this model to ourselves, we can also gain insight into our own behaviour and make positive changes. Overall, the Iceberg Model is a powerful tool for personal growth and building better relationships.

Understanding our basic Needs

AUTONOMY	**CONNECTION**	**HONESTY**
Choice Freedom Independence Space **MEANING** Awareness Celebration of life Discovery Purpose Self-expression Challenge Clarity Effectiveness Growth Stimulation To matter Competence Consciousness Hope Learning Understanding Contribution Creativity Mourning Participation	Acceptance Affection Consideration Consistency Respect / Self-Respect Safety To understand and be understood Appreciation Belonging Empathy Inclusion Security Stability Trust Warmth Cooperation Communication Intimacy Love Support To know and be known Closeness Community Mutuality Nurturing To see and be seen	Authenticity Integrity Presence **PLAY** Joy Humour **PEACE** Beauty Ease Equality Harmony Inspiration Order **PHYSICAL WELL-BEING** Air Food Touch Water Movement Rest Sexual expression Safety Shelter

List of Values

Abundance	Family	Loyalty
Advancement	Finances	Order
Adventure	Finesse	Patience
Affection	Fitness	Patience
Appreciation	Forgiveness	Peace
Balance	Forgiveness	Personal
Be True	Freedom	Development
Beauty	Friendship	Power
Career	Friendship/Relationship	Pride in Your
Caring	Fun	Work
Change	Fun-Loving	Professionalism
Change	Generosity	Prosperity
Charisma	Giving People a Chance	Quality
Clarity	Goodness	Reciprocity
Commonality	Grace	Relationship
Communication	Gratitude	Religion
Compassion	Happiness	Renewal
Connection	Harmony	Respect
Contentment	Home	Respect
Contributing	Honesty	Security
Cooperation	Humanity	Self-Respect
Courage	Humour	Speed
Creativity	Innovation	Spiritualism
Diversity	Integrity	Strength
Effectiveness	Intelligence	Success
Encouragement	Invention	Teamwork
Endurance	Involvement	This Too Shall
Enjoyment	Joy/Play	Pass Attitude
Entertain	Justice	Trusting Your
Entrepreneurial	Kindness	Gut
Excellence	Knowledge	Wealth
Excitement	Leadership	Wellness
Facilitation	Learning	Willingness
Faith	Love	Wisdom
Fame	Love of Career	Work Smarter
		& Harder

CHAPTER 11

Become A Good Self-Observer

"Change the context and change the result"

Self-observation is a key skill for leaders. It involves taking a step back to reflect on actions and tasks. By observing oneself, insights into strengths and areas for improvement can be gained. This self-awareness is essential for making better decisions, improving performance, and ultimately, achieving goals. Leaders who are good self-observers are more adaptable and better equipped to lead effectively in a constantly changing environment.

आप अपने काम के खुद साक्षी बने।

Become a witness to your own work.

Imagine this: you are a leader, and life is a dance floor. Instead of getting lost in the steps of daily tasks, take a balcony break. From up there, you might spot some funny moves you never knew you had! So, get ready to step up and watch your leadership style from a whole new angle.

Why are we talking about the balcony and dance? What is the connection between a leader, dance, and above all, a balcony? You must be having these questions in your mind, and probably even laughing a little bit, but I am about to reveal the significance of the dance and the balcony.

You see, this is an entire concept that will leave you wondering how incredible this is.

Leading from the Balcony: Seeing the Big Picture

Constantly bombarded with tasks and problems can feel like being stuck on a crowded dance floor. There's so much going on around you, that it's hard to see how everything fits together.

But great leaders know how to take a step back from the action and head to the "balcony" for a different perspective. You have to imagine yourself dancing, while you stand on the balcony. The movements, the gestures, the expressions, and the style of your dance; all represent the daily actions and decisions you make as a leader on the "dance floor" below. From the balcony, you can see how these movements (actions) impact the overall flow and success of the dance.

Why Taking a Balcony Break Matters

Imagine working on a giant puzzle, but you're right in the middle of all the pieces. It's hard to see the whole picture and how everything connects, right? That's what it's like to be a leader who never steps back. The world of business is constantly changing, and a plan that seems perfect today might need adjustments tomorrow. Leaders who can adapt quickly are the ones who succeed. By stepping back and looking at the big picture from the balcony, you can see how all the pieces of your organization fit together and make changes as needed. It's like finally stepping back from the puzzle and seeing the beautiful image emerge.

Being Both Active and Reflective

A good leader is both energetic and thoughtful. They can handle the daily tasks that keep things running smoothly (like dancing on the floor). And (like looking out from the balcony) keeping the long-term goals in mind, change your perspective on your dance from your mission and vision angle.

This switch will keep you aligned and the possibility of any failure. Knowing when to do each is a key leadership skill. Think about an athlete - they need to be focused and energetic during the game (dance floor), but they also need to review their performance and strategies afterwards (balcony) to keep improving.

While on the Balcony, Ask Yourself Key Questions

Once you've reached the balcony and have a broader view, ask yourself some important questions to help you make informed decisions:

What's working well?
What are the challenges am I facing now?
What exactly is not working well?
What is needed to solve this problem?
What can be the next?
What exactly do I want to achieve?
How is the connection within the team?
How is every team member working?
What matters most to me/my business/my family?
What lesson did I learn the hard way?

Leading with Wisdom: The Benefits of Taking Balcony Breaks

It's easy to get caught up in the daily grind and forget to take a step back. But the best leaders know that taking time for a "balcony break" is essential for wise decision-making. This time allows them to gain perspective, identify potential problems, and make adjustments to keep their team moving forward, even in times of change. So why not give it a try? Move away from the dance floor for a while and see how the balcony view can help you and your team thrive.

When you're on the balcony, you become an observer. An observer who gains insights, attains the ability to take smarter actions, leading to better results. You reflect on your behaviour and emotions and consider how they influence your actions. Helps you determine that your actions are beneficial and guides you to achieve your goals.

In the last few lines, I refer to the observer. So, it's time to understand what an observer is and how being a good or different observer can change your results

The concepts that I am about to share with all of you lovely readers are OAR and BEL. Let me start with OAR, although, both concepts are interconnected. I will explain how.

Observer->Action->Result (OAR Model)
The fact that the importance of the observer has been made understood, we move to **Action** and **Reaction.**

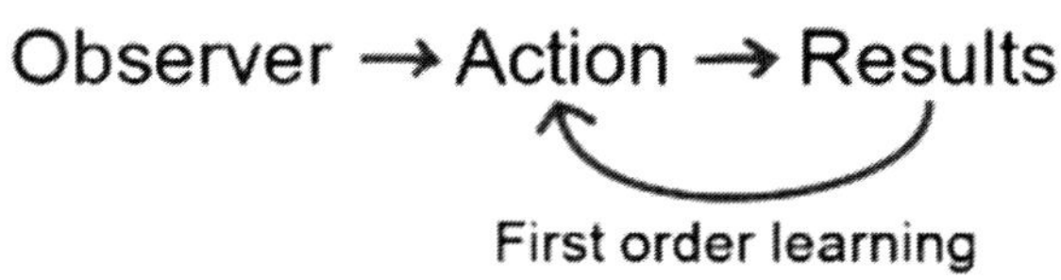

The results we get in life depend on the actions we take. When we don't achieve the desired outcomes, we usually try a different approach. This strategy often works and is known as first-order learning.

Many of the things in life are taught this way. We automatically assume that if we are not getting the results we want, our actions must be incorrect. This assumption is often useful for getting better results. However, sometimes we try every possible action and still don't get the expected results. Or we might follow actions that worked for others but not for us, leaving us puzzled and without the results we seek.

So, when we are not getting the desired results and feel limited in our actions, we should change our perspective. This is known as second-order learning. This is where the observer comes in within the OAR model. The kind of observer you are determines the actions you see as possible, influencing the results you can achieve. By becoming a ***"different observer"*** we open up new possibilities for actions that can lead to the desired result/results.

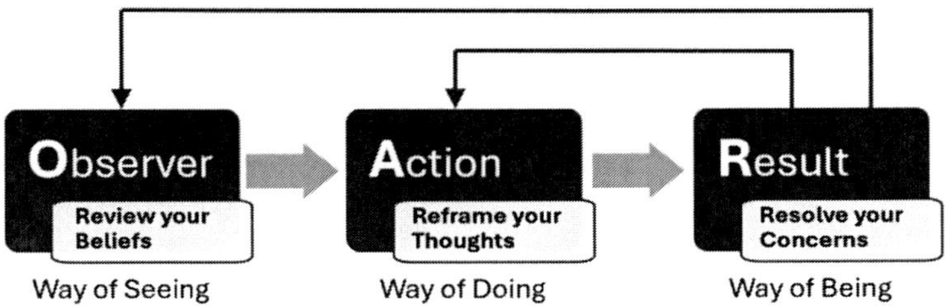

Let's discuss what I meant by a different observer and how being a different observer leads to new actions and new results.

In one of my workshops, I discussed the difference between a manager and a leader. I ask the audience, being you all as leaders, what is it that you feel, your team members are your helping hands OR you are the helping hand of your team? After deep thinking, everyone agreed that to be a good leader they have to be the helping hand of their team, not the vice versa.

Now with changing the whole context, we have to change our belief system that a leader is the helping hand of the team. Now if we refer to the Iceberg model, we learn that beliefs are driving our actions. so, by changing the observer, we change how we see things (beliefs), Which leads to different actions and hence different results.

Taking another example from my experience in the Test-Prep industry, VMC is one of the leading brands in North India for preparation for the IIT-JEE exams. My primary role was HR head, and I was an active member of the strategy management team. To motivate teachers, I used to give them a different context. If someone was not performing, I would explain and re-explain to them give them an insight and make them understand that there is a bigger picture behind your profession. Teaching is a quality, which will define how well the student will learn, effectively defining how well or badly a student will perform in the admission test for IIT or other engineering colleges. So, your teaching should not be just limited to imparting knowledge, but much more than that. I would tell them that your teaching quality will define the base for the whole life/ career of all your students. ***आप उनके भाग्य विधाता हो।*** Which means *'you are the architect of their destiny.'*

Now you can easily imagine how it would impact their belief (how they perceive their job), leading to hidden thoughts and hence actions that lead to different results.

To understand more about how different observer helps you get different results, we need to go through with BEL model.

The BEL Model has three aspects of our state of being (Body, Emotions & Language). These three aspects affect the way we see different things, which I referred to above as observer. In this section, I am going to explain

1. What do we mean by Body, Emotion & Language?
2. How do Body, Emotions and Language (BEL) have an effect on context (how we perceive / how we see)?
3. How does being a different observer (exploring how we see things), change in the context of what we are doing, align the BEL aspects?
4. How to change the context?

What do we mean by Body, Emotion & Language and Context

Body: Different Body Disposition

Leadership is often viewed as a purely mental exercise – strategic thinking, decision-making, and communication. However, emerging research suggests that our physicality plays a crucial role in effective leadership. This concept focuses on **body dispositions**, which are unconscious tendencies in how we hold and move our bodies that can influence our leadership style and impact others. Understanding these dispositions can empower leaders to become more mindful and impactful.

To understand the language of the body, we need to understand the four body dispositions. After explaining the BEL model, we will discuss body disposition in detail.

Emotions

As we have learned in the previous chapter about emotions, let's recap briefly with a simple example, consider a situation where a customer service representative is handling a difficult client. If the representative views the client as a challenge to overcome rather than an angry individual, they are more likely to remain calm and find a solution. This shift in perspective, influenced by emotions, can lead to more effective actions and outcomes. Therefore, emotions are integral to our decision-making and actions.

Language

This includes both the words we speak and the thoughts that we carry in our minds. These thoughts are like our inner language, shaping how we perceive the world and communicate with others. For example, when we think about a past event or plan for the future, we're using this inner language. We also discussed that these thoughts/stories (language) about past or future affects our behaviour.

Context / Observer

The context gives the purpose or meaning to what you are doing. It changes the way we see. When this purpose is clear, you get more aligned towards the same. You just need to understand the power of context, and how changing the way we see our goals impacts your results.

A context is literally created by creating it and it cannot be created from outside or someone else. You yourself have the power to create the context for your life/job etc.

Now, as you know the power of context, create the context of your own and see how it benefits you in your actions and results.

How Body, Emotions and Language (BEL) affects context (how we perceive / how we see)

Together these three aspects (BEL) define the way we see things, these three are very much bundled with each other. By bundled, I mean if you change one of them, it will align the other two and it will change the type of observer we are.

For example, in the chapter on positive thinking, we discussed that when we want to start something new, we have positive and negative thoughts. If our mind is strong, we nurture more positive thoughts.

Before I share how these positive thoughts affect your emotions and body state, I will suggest you first try to bring some positive thoughts for any of your current problems and see how it affects your emotional and body state.

Everyone can have different changes in emotion and body state as per their case. Let me share with you my emotions and body state, say when I get positive thoughts "Yes, I can do it". The emotions, I can sense now are Empowered, safe, eager. The change in the body state is, that my energy is moving in all directions, and it is more flexible now to leap out into new prodigies.

Another example is in some of the transformational programs, the facilitator asks the audience to draw and colour whatever they want to. The audience spent say an hour on draw/colour as per their choice. As an outcome, they feel relaxed and helps them increase their focus. In this case, what the facilitator did, with drawing as a tool, he changed the body state to "Open or Resolute", as per the case. By changing the body state, the emotions and thoughts get changed.

With the above two examples, any change in any of these 3 states (Body, Emotions & Language) changes other states. And they together define our way of seeing (perspective/context), which we are calling as observers.

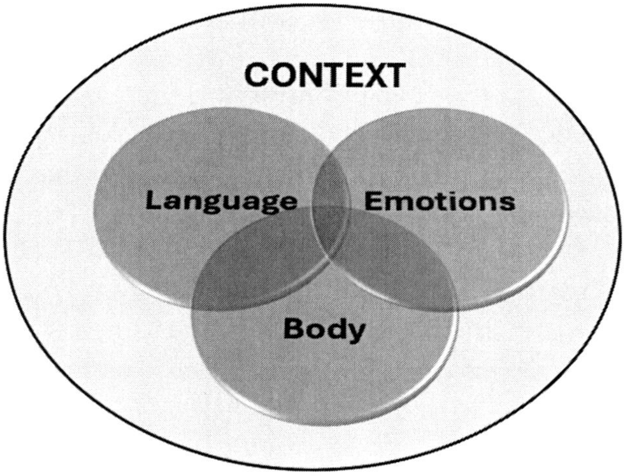

How being a different observer (exploring how we see things) and changing in the context of what we are doing, aligns the BEL aspects.

In the OAR model, we discussed examples, where we changed the context. One of the examples was where we are saying a leader is a helping hand to the team. Similarly, we discussed the difference in how we see things when we call a wife (who is not into any job/self-employed) as a homemaker instead of a housewife. Now BEL model is in place, try to be a different observer by taking any of the above examples.

Does being a different observer, produce any change in your Body or emotional or Language aspect of it? The moment you consider yourself as a helping hand to your team, your thoughts(language) change immediately, it also affects your body and emotional aspects. The bigger you create your context, you will find more energy in your body, there will be more positive thoughts in your mind and more strong and positive emotions. All BEL aspects will get aligned on its own to your context. So, the moment you change the context (way of seeing), you will notice your actions (way of doing) will change and hence the result/outcome will change.

There may be times when your body is giving a different message than your thoughts. This is the time when all three aspects of BEL are not aligned. Whenever you find yourself in this stage, it is a message that you are not clear of your context, or you are not conscious of your context. And recreate your context to change the actions and hence results

Different Body Dispositions

Here's a breakdown of the four body dispositions in leadership:

1. **Resolute Disposition**

Focus: Forward Momentum and Direction

This disposition embodies a **goal-oriented** leader. Their body language reflects a **determined** and **assertive** approach. Imagine a leader leaning forward, with a focused gaze, conveying a clear sense of purpose and direction.

2. **Openness or Open Disposition**

Focus: Receptiveness and Invitation

An open leader fosters **collaboration** and **inclusivity.** Their body language projects a **calm** and **approachable** demeanour. Think of a leader leaning back slightly with open arms, creating a welcoming and receptive space for others.

3. **Flexible Disposition**

Focus: Adaptability and Openness to Change

Flexible leaders are **agile** and can adjust to new situations. Their body language reflects **dynamism** and **enthusiasm.** Imagine a leader with an open posture, perhaps gesturing or moving their body slightly, demonstrating a willingness to embrace new ideas.

4. **Stable Disposition**

Focus: Composure and Groundedness

Stable leaders inspire **trust** and **reliability.** Their body language conveys **steadiness** and **control.** Imagine a leader with a solid posture and minimal unnecessary movement, projecting a sense of calm and unwavering focus even in challenging situations.

5. **Centred**

Focus: Centered, relaxed, calm

Let's explore the concept of the CENTER, a neutral state that allows us to transition to any of the four body dispositions. Being in the CENTER is our fundamental and stable state as human beings. It means having an awareness of our bodily sensations. Are we feeling tense or relaxed? Are we experiencing heat or cold? Are we balanced or unsteady?

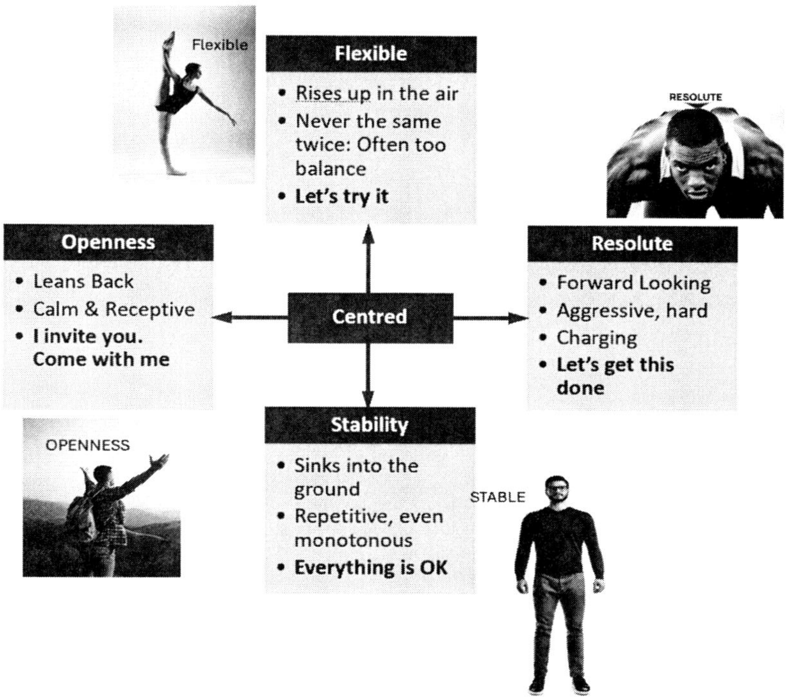

By understanding these dispositions and how they manifest in our bodies, leaders can leverage them to **strengthen their communication**, **inspire their teams**, and **navigate complex situations** with greater effectiveness.

The OAR Model (Observer-Action-Results) explains how our way of being (Kind of observer we are) determines the results we seek and the actions we can imagine achieving those results. Your observer is your unique perspective—the lens through which you see the situation. It encompasses your beliefs, assumptions, and emotional state.

When we encounter problems, we often assume that adjusting our actions will solve them. This is called first-order learning—trying different actions until we achieve the desired outcome. However, sometimes our attempts fall short. This is where the observer becomes critical. The observer you are shapes the possibilities for action you can perceive. Moreover, your observer infuses purpose into your actions, making them effective. Taking the correct action without a meaningful perspective may lead to suboptimal results. So, when faced with challenges, consider second-order learning—trying a different observer.

Now, let's explore the BEL Model (Body-Emotions-Language). The interplay between body, emotions, and language matters. Pay attention to your physical state (body), as it affects communication and well-being. Emotions influence your leadership effectiveness. Finally, language—how you express yourself—shapes team dynamics and organizational culture. Integrating these elements leads to authentic and impactful leadership.

When we shift our perspective as an observer, it naturally aligns our body, emotions, and language with the new context.

In summary, understanding both the OAR and BEL models empowers leaders to navigate complexity, adapt actions, and create meaningful results by integrating their internal state with their external behaviour.

CHAPTER 12

Working With Empathy

"Something not right does not mean it is wrong"

The depth and magnanimity of your power lie in your empathy towards the people you deal with.
Something not right does not mean it is wrong. It may be right for someone else.

The above-mentioned quote is very close to my heart and all these years I, as a professional, have built my core and my success rests on the foundation of being empathetic.

So, to procure the highest level of output, in terms of results, all a leader needs to do is connect with his/her team on an emotional level first. If you can do that, you have won the better part of the battle. Empathy is a tool that is of extreme significance because an individual who has empathy, truly respects the emotions of people around, is equipped with the trait of a winner. It also speaks volumes of that individual's self-esteem and pride.

When empathy is understood intricately by a leader, the stress factor in the boss-worker relationship gets released. What emerges is sincere faith, respect, and trust towards the leader. Once this stage is attained, no assignment/task will ever seem impossible to achieve. An empathetic leader can keep their team motivated, and march ahead with confidence, only to achieve immeasurable heights.

So, **what is empathy?** It's the ability to understand another person's thoughts and feelings in a situation from their point of view, rather than your own. It differs from sympathy, where one is moved by the thoughts and feelings of another but maintains an emotional distance.

How to build it?

Empathy doesn't come naturally for everyone. When I say, "To be empathetic, you must be empathetic," I mean that empathy goes beyond mere words. It involves truly putting yourself in another person's shoes and feeling their emotions as if they were your own. It's about recognising that two people can both be right; it's not just a logical understanding, but a psychological one.

Practicing empathy is a conscious choice, and the more we do it, the more intuitive it becomes.
Follow this quote,

"If you have to choose between what is right and what is kind; always choose what is kind because that will always be right."

Empathy is also keeping the balance of decision-making through the mind and with the heart. So, you need to learn to listen to both and make the balance of it.

The following are a few traits that define an empathetic leader:

- Approachable.
- Takes care of team members.
- Involve others in the conversation.
- Flexible.
- Motivates and empowers their team.

To be an empathetic leader, it is essential to develop specific habits and practices. here's how you can cultivate empathy in your leadership:

1. **Be non-judgemental:** Challenge your assumptions. avoid jumping to conclusions and try to see situations from different perspectives.
2. **Listen actively:** don't just hear someone's story - feel it. Engage fully with what the other person is saying, showing that you value their experiences.
3. **Seek feedback:** Seeking feedback also demonstrates that you are humble, open-minded, and willing to grow as a leader. You can seek feedback from your team members, peers, mentors, or coaches, and use it as an opportunity to practice empathy and gratitude.
4. **Express empathy:** Show that you care about your team's feelings and experience. If you make a mistake, acknowledge it and apologize sincerely.
5. **Practice self-empathy:** Recognise and accept your own feelings and needs without judgement or criticism. Being mindful of your inner state and forgiving towards yourself can improve your resilience and authenticity.
6. **Be there to support your team:** Sometimes all a leader needs to evaluate is the need for extending a helping hand. Be it a fresh perspective or practical assistance, just say, "I'm here to offer my support in any way I can." Once this is said, there is an instant relief, and the person feels completely connected.

Remember, you can't serve from an Empty cup. kindness must start with you. To be empathetic, one needs to be empathetic to themselves first. This may seem a little new but let me explain it for your clarity.

The key to success might lie in a surprising place: self-compassion. it's not about weakness, but about reading yourself with the same kindness you would offer a friend. This simple act unlocked a powerful leadership style.

Self-compassionate leaders have a heightened sense of self-awareness. They can identify their strengths and weaknesses clearly, allowing them to make sound decisions and continuously improve. This approach also stimulates resilience. When faced with setbacks, they remain positive and bounce back quickly, providing crucial stability for their teams during challenging times.

Trust is another benefit. Self-compassion translates to authenticity, making leaders more approachable and fostering a strong connection with their team members. People are naturally drawn to those they feel they can relate to, leading to a more trusting and collaborative work environment.
Furthermore, self-compassion helps prevent burnout. Leaders who prioritise their own well-being set a positive example for the teams, promoting a healthy work-life balance and a more sustainable work culture. Finally, self-compassionate leaders Excel at navigating conflict. Their ability to see things from different perspectives allows them to find balanced solutions and handle disagreements fairly. Therefore, leading with kindness isn't a concession, it's a strategic advantage. It nurtures happier, more effective leaders who can build strong, resilient teams capable of overcoming any obstacle.

How does it help in managing people?

My philosophy suggests that everyone behaves similarly in a given scenario. By putting yourself in the second person's shoes and understanding their background and experiences, you can get a deep understanding of the root cause of their behaviour. This approach allows you to empathise with them more effectively, gaining insights into their motivations, fears, and aspirations.

Understanding the underlying causes of behaviour enables you to identify solutions that address the main issues, rather than just the symptoms. This can lead to more effective conflict resolution, better decision-making, a more supportive and inclusive work environment, and overall improved team performance.

An empathetic leader goes beyond surface explanations when tasks are incomplete. instead of jumping to conclusions, they investigate the underlying reasons, which can lead to more effective solutions and a supportive approach. They have to drill down to understand and get to the bottom of the situation. It is only after this will they be able to understand the following:

1. Intention or attitude: an empathetic leader considers whether the action is intentional or if there is a problem with the attitude.
2. Is there a lethargic or laid-back approach?
3. Effort vs outcome: they assess if the individual puts in 100% effort, yet the results are not up to the mark.

If a leader reprimands a team member in scenario 3, it would be wrong. Considering the team members' emotions is crucial. The team member/members might already be feeling bad about the situation, so scolding them could make them feel even worse. An empathetic action would be to support and guide them through the issue, rather than criticising them.

As we summarise the chapter on empathy, let us look at the key aspects.

- Leaders must ensure that the desired outcome is achieved while also meeting the interests of team members and stakeholders.
- Empathy is essential for leaders to create win win situations.
- "To be empathetic, you must be empathetic" Means that empathy involves more than just words.; It's about truly putting yourself in another person's shoes and understanding what they are experiencing.
- By empathising, leaders can grasp the background and cause of others' actions or behaviours.
- While leaders already understand their own challenges and organisational needs, empathy helps them see the other person's perspective as well.
- With a comprehensive understanding of both sides of a problem, leaders can make decisions that are beneficial for everyone involved.

RECAP

Recap and What's More

So far, you would have understood that to be a great leader, you must transform yourself. The knowledge I have shared so far with you in this book focuses on self-transformation.

We've discussed core skills related to leadership at a subtle level. In the second part of this book, I will cover tools and knowledge closely linked to vital leadership skills. Before I jump into that, I would like to recap what we have learned so far and relate different concepts with a context.

First, we have learned that change is going to happen. Everyone should be aware that change is inevitable and quickly identify and adapt to it. This is especially important for leaders, as they are responsible for the organization's goals, growth, and the work of team members. Leaders must not only be personally ready for change but also help their team members to be ready for changes.

I also emphasised the importance and relevance of your team trusting you. To earn their trust, you must align with your ethical values. Trust is a mutual element; It must flow both ways.

Then, we learned a basic tool to deep dive into (Decode Your Mind) to learn how to zoom in on any incident, situation, or work you perform to get a clear picture of the background. We used this simple deep dive skill to understand the bigger picture (the context/purpose) of our day-to-day activities and this change in understanding context makes a big difference.

We utilised this straightforward deep dive technique to grasp the broader context and purpose of our daily activities. This shift in understanding significantly impacts are approach and outcomes.

After this, we talked about the difference between a manager and a leader. I hope this was an eye-opener and that you learned many things that will help you transform from a manager to a leader.

The rest of the chapters focus on building Emotional Intelligence. The key component a leader has to work on is emotional intelligence (EI). We discussed the concept of EI, which has five components: self-awareness, self-regulation, motivation, empathy, and social skills.

Many times, you will find the buzzword EQ (Emotional Quotient), which is simply a way to express someone's rating on EI. Everything we learned was aimed at improving your EQ. Let me relate EI with our learning so far:

Concepts like positive thinking and a winning spirit are useful for the self-motivation component of EI.

Being non-judgmental is the foundation of EI and great leadership. Judgmental statements lead to conflict and aggression, so being non-judgmental helps a leader avoid such tough scenarios and fosters better relationships. It creates a space for a leader to think in all possible ways, aiding in self-awareness and self-regulation. Empathy can only develop if we have the space created by being non-judgmental.

We then learned to identify and express our emotions. Honestly, it's not difficult to understand our emotions, but we haven't learned or practised this due to how we were raised.

Referring to a list helps us relate to our emotions, and we also learn to focus on the intensity of these emotions. Understanding emotions helps with self-awareness. We also learned the ICEBERG concept to deep dive into understanding our behaviour and emotions. Creating an iceberg for your behaviour helps with self-awareness, and dissolving the iceberg or breaking the belief is a tool for self-regulation.

Once you learn/practice identifying and expressing your emotions, it will transform you to understand other people's emotions too, leading to being more empathetic.

We discussed the OAR & BEL model in one of the latest chapters. We learned to step back and be a different observer, seeing the bigger context. By changing the context, we can change our BEL and hence our actions to achieve better results. Being a good observer means observing oneself. When you practice self-observation, you become more aware of yourself. As awareness increases, you understand your strengths, weaknesses, and areas for improvement. These concepts (being in the balcony, OAR, BEL model) help with self-awareness and self-regulation.

The following table shows the tools we have learnt and how it is useful to build EQ.

Tools learnt	Awareness	Regulation	Motivation	Empathy
Deep-Dive	◎	◎		◎
Positive Thinking & Winning Spirit			●	
Iceberg - Understand your behaviour	●			◎
Dissolve - Iceberg		●		
Non-Judgmental				●
Identify & Expressing Your Emotions	●	◎		
Beneath Emotion there is a Need	●			●
Adaptive Challenge do not have Yes/No				◎
Don't find intention in mistakes - Forgiveness				◎
Balcony & Dance	◎			
OAR-BEL Model	●	◎		

It would be fair to say, that all of the above is a simple recap that has taught us to be more self-observant, and increased the awareness that allowed us to continually improve and climb up the ladder to becoming a good leader. It has also taught us that as you develop the above skills, you will not only enhance but also inspire and guide your teams towards greater success.

CHAPTER 13

Leadership Styles & Situation based Leadership

"To choose the best, you need to know all the options"

On a lighter note, leadership styles are like flavours of ice cream—each one offers something different and enjoyable. Understanding these styles can be as fun as trying out new ice cream flavours, helping leaders find the perfect "flavour" for their team and situation.

Before diving into the various leadership styles, let's first discuss the two key aspects that define them.

Firstly, there's a common misconception that a leader's behaviour determines their leadership style. For instance, a demanding person might be thought to naturally adopt a directive leadership style. However, this is a myth. The reality is that leadership styles are not predetermined by a leader's behaviour; instead, they are determined by the situation at hand. leadership is not a one-size-fits-all concept. Different challenges call for different leadership styles, highlighting the need for leaders to be adaptable and versatile. There can be various types of situations/contexts and a leader cannot falter.

Second aspect to understand:

'Leaders often develop a recipe for success based on past experiences, but when the context shifts, applying the same recipe can lead to failure.'

Because change is constant, each situation can vary significantly. Leadership style that was effective before may not work every time. Each scenario is unique and requires a tailored approach to manage it effectively.

Just as engineering views objects from various perspectives like top, bottom, and side views to understand a 3D object in 2D, we must also understand leadership styles from different angles to adapt to varying situations. Each perspective offers a unique insight into how leadership skills are defined.

Layman's style to understand Leadership styles:
From a layman's point of view, how can we differentiate between two leaders?
The first few instincts or questions that pop up are:

1. How do they adapt to change?
2. How do they delegate tasks?
3. How do they provide feedback to a team?
4. How do they support the team's development?
5. How do they facilitate high-level goals?
6. How do they motivate the team members?

Leadership styles based on action orientations:
We have three action orientations; **Analytical, Contextual, and Relational.** Each orientation type exhibits general characteristics, strengths, and weaknesses and needs to be managed and communicated with in different ways. Based on this orientation we have leadership style
Now, let me give you a brief description of all action orientation-based style:

1. ANALYTICAL LEADERS: These leaders are data-driven. They prefer to base their decisions on concrete information rather than gut feelings, or instincts. They rely heavily on data analysis, models, and metrics to formulate their plans. They firmly believe that a well-informed decision is more likely to lead to success.
2. CONTEXTUAL LEADERS: Contextual leaders look beyond the immediate task or problem at hand. They consider the broader context in which the situation exists.

This includes factors such as market conditions, competitor strategies, and overall industry trends. They believe that understanding the context is imperative for making effective decisions.

3. RELATIONAL LEADERS: Relational leaders focus on relationships and how their actions will impact others. They consider the dynamics between people, power, structures, social networks, and the personal feelings and motivations of those involved. They believe that building strong relationships and understanding interpersonal dynamics is key to achieving their goals.

We can differentiate leadership style with various dimensions. Leaders can be optimistic, pessimistic, or realistic., each bringing a unique perspective to opportunities and challenges. They may also choose micro-management, closely overseeing tasks, or macro-management, focussing on big-picture goals. While some may adopt a directive approach, giving clear instructions, or a supportive approach, prioritising team well-being and development. Understanding these traits and styles helps in effectively managing and adapting to different situations.

Let's explorer different leadership styles with a broader perspective.

There are six different leadership styles that we will explore in this topic. Each style has its own unique approach to leading and managing people. From leaders who demand immediate compliance to those who develop people for the future, understanding these styles can help in recognizing and adapting to different leadership methods.

They are:

- **Coercive** Leaders demand immediate compliance
- **Authoritative** leaders mobilize people toward a vision.
- **Affiliative** Leaders create emotional bonds and harmony

- **Democratic** Leaders build consensus through participation
- **Pacesetting** leaders expect excellence and self-direction
- **Coaching** leaders develop people for the future

1. **Coercive Leadership** is a kind of commanding leadership where leaders make the key decision with very limited input from the team. Team members are told what to do and how to do it. In this, fear is the key motivation. As involvement of employees is low and hence it has low employee satisfaction/motivation.
2. **Authoritative Leaders** is also known as Transformational" / "Visionary" leadership where the leader delegates the tasks with proper authority and empowerment to achieve the task. He Sets forth an inspiring vision of the future and also helps staff see how their work will contribute to a better world. This style motivates and excites the employee.
3. **Affiliative Leaders** focus on doing things which is good for all. He takes care of employees and receives strong loyalty in back. Leaders build teams to ensure followers are connected and hence employees feel like part of the family. It helps in healing organizations with serious divisions, conflicts or broken trust and it produces happier workers
4. **Democratic Leaders** create participation through consensus and seek input from key people on important decisions. He listens carefully to concerns. The collective decision was strengthened by buy-in and commitment across the organization.
5. **Pacesetting Leaders** hold high standards - for self & organization. They are useful to get quick results from a highly motivated team and always demand faster, better performance. It creates pressure for immediate results may restrict creativity, and innovation and micromanagement erode trust, and stunts development.

6. **Coaching Leaders** invest in the personal development of the staff by asking questions like." What is the purpose of your job or your life?", or "How can you do this better"? or "What are the consequences if you work in a particular way?". These questions help the team understand their professional and personal goals. The leader focuses on getting the best out of the key team members.

Which Leadership Style is the best?

The answer is: it depends!

Which style to adopt, does not depend on the leader's basic nature but depends on the situation. For example, if there is a fire on the floor, will a leader act as dictator OR will be democratic?

Obviously, in this case leader has to be coercive.

To continue which style to go for, we need to understand leadership styles are not a set of rules but see it as a tailored approach based on the situation. The best leadership style is the one that matches the needs of the person (team member) working with you.

To explain this statement, we need to first explore the following:

1) What are responsibilities of a leader?
2) How leaders provide support to their team member?
3) How to define the skill-will Level (how much can you be dependent on a person) of team member?

And then, we will relate support styles with skill-will level.

What are the responsibilities of a leader?

A leader's primary responsibility is to ensure their team works as effectively as they would themselves. This involves understanding team expectations, tracking performance, and providing the necessary guidance based on team members' skills.

How do leaders provide support to their team member?

Leaders are the helping hand to their team to accomplish their assigned tasks or responsibilities. There are two different ways, he supports or influence his team:

1) Directive Behaviour: It is related to the task. It is about what, how and when things are to be done.
2) Supportive Behaviour: It is related to the person, building the trust & respect, team motivation and confidence.

A leader typically balances directing and supporting their team, adjusting their approach based on their team's skill levels and the task at hand. Depending on which approach is more dominant, there are four stages or levels that describe how a leader behaves at each stage.

Stage	Supportive / Directive	Leaders Behaviour
L1	High-Directive, Low-Supportive	Telling, Directing, or Guiding
L2	High-Directive, High-Supportive	Selling, Coaching, or Explaining
L3	High-Supportive, Low-Directive	Participating, Facilitating, or Collaborating
L4	Low-Directive, Low-Supportive	Delegating, Empowering, or Monitoring

Skill-Will Level of team member

There are two key aspects based on which a leader decides to what extent he needs to depend on his team member's:

1) Skill: Domain Experience / Knowledge
2) Will: Behaviour & Commitment Level

The following table defines four Skill-Will level's (SWL) based on the above-mentioned aspects.

	Behaviour / Commitment Level	
Domain Experience	High	Moderate
Low Experienced	SW1	SW1
Low–Moderate Experience	SW2	SW1
Moderate–High Experience	SW3	SW2
Expert	SW4	SW3

Since a person's expertise can vary across different types of tasks, an individual might have different levels of Skill-Will for different tasks.

Mapping Support Styles with Skill-Will Levels.

No single leadership style is inherently better than another. Success depends on matching the leadership style to the employee's skill-will levels.

The following illustrates the relationship between Support Styles and Skill-Will Levels.

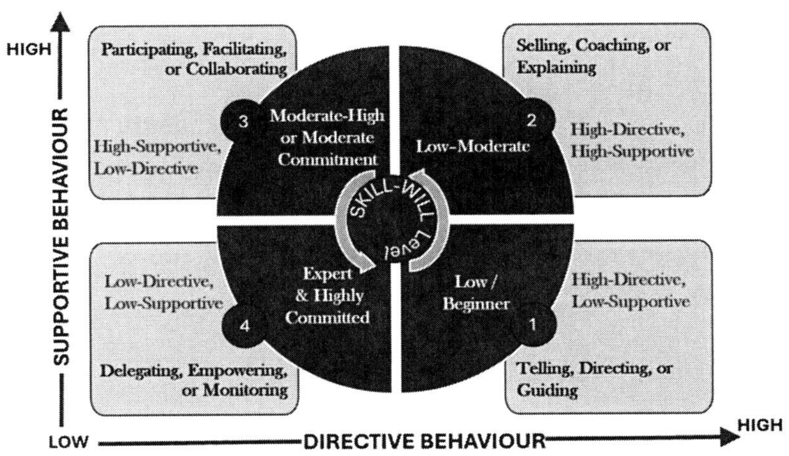

- **We can differentiate a leadership style in various dimensions**:
    - Analytical, Contextual, and Relational Leaders
    - Optimistic, pessimistic, or realistic leaders
    - Micro-management vs Macro-management Style
    - Directive Vs Supportive Leaders

- We can define the **leader based on fixed styles** in the following ways:
    - **Coercive** Leaders demand immediate compliance
    - **Authoritative** leaders mobilize people toward a vision
    - **Affiliative** Leaders create emotional bonds and harmony
    - **Democratic** Leaders build consensus through participation
    - **Pace setting** leaders expect excellence and self-direction

- **Situation based leadership approach**

Skill-Will Level	Supportive or Directive	Leaders Behaviour
SW1 Low dependency	High-Directive, Low-Supportive	Telling, Directing, or Guiding
SW2 Low-Moderate	High-Directive, High-Supportive	Selling, Coaching, or Explaining
SW3 Moderate-High	High-Supportive, Low-Directive	Participating, Facilitating, or Collaborating
SW4 Highly dependable	Low-Directive, Low-Supportive	Delegating, Empowering, or Monitoring

CHAPTER 14

Motivating Your Team Members

"Motivate people with more responsibilities rather than money"

What is employee motivation? If I get to answer this question, I will say: It is the spark that excites someone to start their workday. It's what fuels their enthusiasm and dedication. When employees see themselves and the company as one, their motivation soars to a different level. In other words, we aim for our team to treat the organisation as their own.

A true leader ignites their team's passion and enthusiasm. They make people feel valued by investing time in understanding their priorities, strengths, and needs. A leader can only motivate others if they are motivated themselves, making it crucial for leaders to stay inspired. Motivated leaders appreciate hard work and encourage their team's potential through meaningful and enjoyable challenges and goals.

So, the first step towards motivating the team is the Leader's Self-Motivation.

To maintain ongoing motivation, we must first understand what drives the motivator. It's not just about money, as you'll come to see. Many time-tested theories and principles have been adapted to keep teams motivated. This requires a sharp mind, dedication, and a genuine desire for team growth.

Fear is not a sustainable motivator. While fear might push people to complete tasks in the short term, it fails to produce lasting results. In the past, fear of job loss could make people work, but times and philosophies have changed.

Cash incentives aren't always effective either. When rewards are monetary, the leader is often motivated, not the team. Incentive-based motivation is like pulling the team forward, while fear push from behind.

So, what truly keeps a team motivated? Good pay and a pleasant work environment can keep them satisfied, but not necessarily motivated. It's important to distinguish between factors that prevent dissatisfaction and those that drive motivation.

To explore this further, let's discuss a popular theory that clarifies this distinction.

Herzberg's Motivation Theory:
This is based on two different human needs. One set of needs comes from our basic biological drives, like hunger, which creates a need to earn money. these are known as hygiene factors.
The other set of needs is tied to our unique human ability to achieve and grow psychologically. these are known as motivating factors.

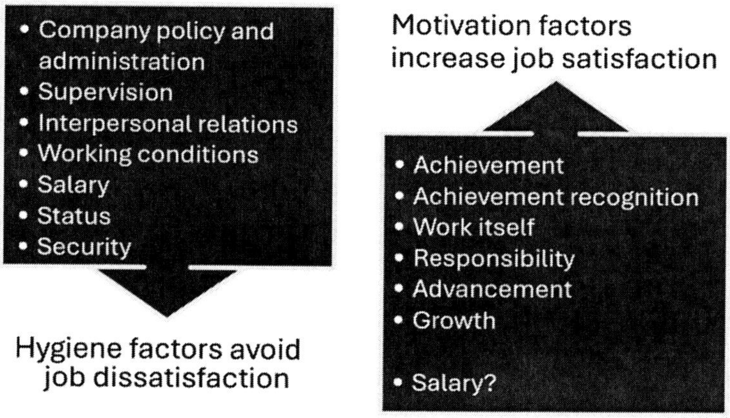

The image depicts Herzberg's two-factor theory, which proposes that two independent factors influence an individual's job satisfaction and motivation: hygiene factors and motivation factors.

- **Hygiene factors**, also known as dissatisfiers, relate to the job environment and can lead to dissatisfaction if absent but don't necessarily lead to satisfaction if present. These include aspects like company policy, supervision, salary, and working conditions.
- **Motivation factors**, also known as satisfiers, are those that are related to the job itself and are more likely to contribute to job satisfaction. These include factors like achievement, recognition, advancement, growth, and responsibility.

Hygiene factors include:

Company policies: These should be fair and clear to every employee. They must also be equivalent to those of competitors.

Supervision: Supervision must be fair and appropriate. The employee should be given as much autonomy as is reasonable.

Relationships: There should be no tolerance for bullying or cliques. A healthy, amiable, and appropriate relationship should exist between peers, superiors, and subordinates.

Work conditions: Equipment and the working environment should be safe, fit for purpose, and hygienic.

Salary: The pay structure should be fair and reasonable. It should also be competitive with other organizations in the same industry.

Status: The organization should maintain the status of all employees within the organization.

Security: It is important that employees feel that their job is secure, and they are not under the constant threat of being laid off.

Motivating factors include:

Achievement: A job must give an employee a sense of achievement. This will provide a proud feeling of having done something difficult but worthwhile.

Recognition: A job must provide an employee with praise and recognition of their successes. This recognition should come from both their superiors and their peers.

The work itself: The job itself must be interesting, and varied, and provide enough of a challenge to keep employees motivated.

Responsibility: Employees should "own" their work. They should hold themselves responsible for this completion and not feel as though they are being micromanaged.

Advancement: Promotion opportunities should exist for the employee.

Growth: The job should allow employees to learn new skills. This can happen either on the job or through more formal training.

In the context of the theory, we discussed earlier, it's important to understand that being dissatisfied does not necessarily mean being satisfied or motivated.

Let me explain the same through the following diagram

Consider a large corporation with excellent infrastructure and facilities, offering everything an employee could desire. While one might assume that employees there would be fully satisfied, the question arises: would everyone be equally motivated? This scenario illustrates the distinction between satisfaction and motivation.

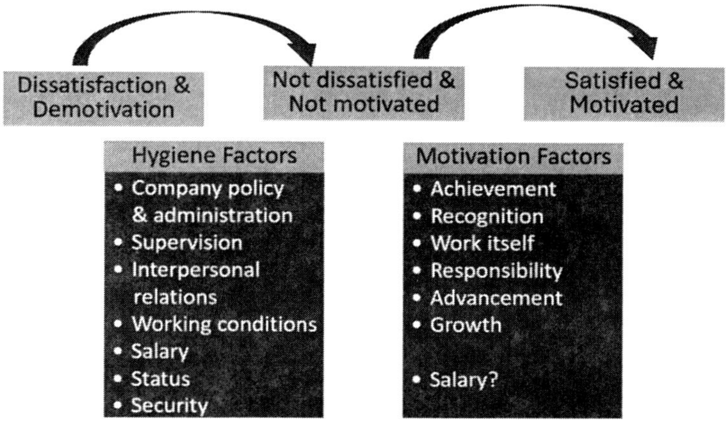

I'll share my own experience to illustrate this point further. When I worked at Cadence, a renowned software development company known for its exceptional work environment, I felt overwhelmed and fully satisfied in terms of hygiene factors such as infrastructure, facilities, policies, and processes. The company was even awarded "The Best Company" by a renowned survey company while I was there.

Despite the excellent hygiene factors, I didn't feel truly satisfied. I eventually left Cadence to join Nagarro Software, a much smaller company at the time, with around 300-400 employees. Nagarro was not as strong in terms of hygiene factors, and work-life balance was challenging. However, I consider my time at Nagarro to be the golden period of my career.

The difference was like the work. At Cadence, although I had a good salary and excellent infrastructure, the work was not challenging. I had concerns about my market value decreasing due to the lack of challenging work. I often likened my situation to being a dog travelling in a big luxury car—comfortable, but not fulfilling.

On the other hand, at Nagarro, despite the demanding work and the company's smaller size, I thoroughly enjoyed my eight years there. I rapidly progressed in my career, jumping four levels in four years. When I left Cadence in 2006, I was part of a small team of 2-3 people, leading projects. By 2010-11, at Nagarro, I was a functional head, leading a team of around 250 people.

These examples highlight that while I was not dissatisfied with Cadence (due to its excellent hygiene factors), I was not truly satisfied or motivated because of the nature of my work. Conversely, at Nagarro, despite the challenges, I was much more satisfied and motivated because of the meaningful work and rapid career growth.
Now, there is a significant point that we have understood:

NOT DISSATISFIED DOES NOT MEAN SATISFIED (MOTIVATED)

Motivation comes from the job itself: Forget fancy perks! The most important factors lie in the work itself. A challenging job with opportunities for growth and personal satisfaction is key.

Now let us discuss these motivational factors in more detail.

1. **Give your employees more ownership/authority:** This can involve loosening control while still holding them accountable, giving them broader tasks or complete projects, introducing tougher challenges, and letting them specialise in areas of interest. This empowers them to use their skills and grow in their roles.
2. In the last chapter, we discussed the skill levels. **Helping employees to transform** from Level 1 to Level 4, which helps them in their growth and level of involvement in the work they do, keeps them motivated.

3. Giving a person a **Complete unit of work** (say one department, one module, are or so on).
4. Assigning individuals specific or specialised tasks that will enable them to **Become experts** in what they are doing.
5. **Involve people in decision making:** As a leader, you want employees to treat the organisation as their own company, but do you involve employees in decision-making, say in goal setting for them?

   To increase the teams' commitment and ownership, a leader must involve them in decision-making as much as possible. We should keep our process fair and should be explained well at all levels of the organisation as per the case.
6. **Making periodic reports directly available to team** rather than to just with team leads. This gives a feeling of recognition to the team members. They feel integral part of the team.
7. A **leader's increased confidence** in the team allows for greater delegation and fuels individual motivation among team members.
8. Ethical, values of organisations and leaders make employees feel proud and motivated to be a part of something meaningful. This alignment with personal values fosters trust, respect and a sense of purpose, enhancing job satisfaction and commitment.
9. **The Organization culture around EI & Empathy:** Organisations that emphasise emotional intelligence (EI) and empathy create a supportive work environment. Prioritising EI helps leaders manage emotions and connect with others, while empathy strengthens relationships. Employee-centric policies and equitable decision-making ensure fairness and well-being, resulting in a motivated and committed workforce.

I believe you got the idea of how to motivate employees

Coming to the main point, i.e., "Money." Is it a hygiene factor/motivational factor?
Can you give more money even with a smaller number of Roles and Responsibilities?
Even with more money, with less work, make employees secure?

Money, in the context of motivation, acts more as a hygiene than a direct motivator. While offering more money with reduced responsibility might seem attractive on the surface, it can lead to decreased engagement and a sense of stagnation

Let us analyse it from a business perspective: From a business standpoint, simply throwing money at employees without greater contributions isn't a sustainable strategy. While a company may have the financial resources to do so in the short term, true employee satisfaction and motivation stem from fulfilling and challenging work. An employee whose salary significantly outpaces their role's responsibilities may experience job insecurity, leading to fear-driven work rather than genuine motivation.

If you still see money as a motivation factor, then see it from the perspective that if a leader has groomed a team member with a better job, which leads to more salary/money actually creates motivation. Money alone cannot be a motivation.

In my previous example, at Cadence, despite good pay and facilities, the job lacked challenge, leading to low motivation. This shows money alone doesn't compensate for job dissatisfaction.

In essence, while money is important, it is not the primary motivator for most individuals. Job enrichment, personal growth, and a sense of accomplishment are often more powerful drivers of motivation and satisfaction in the long run.

"Not dissatisfied does not mean satisfied (motivated)"

The key to motivating employees isn't just about surroundings, but about the work itself. People are most motivated by jobs that challenge them, offer opportunities to learn and grow, and are interesting to them.

Hygiene factors like company policies, supervision, relationships, work conditions, salary, status, and security are related to basic human needs and help to not feel dissatisfied.

Motivators (sometimes called 'satisfiers') are those factors directly concerned with the satisfaction gained from a job, such as:

- Sense of achievement and value: Feeling like their work matters and seeing results keeps them wanting to do more. Completing a challenging task is a great motivator!
- Recognition: A simple "thank you" goes a long way! Public recognition by colleagues or managers can boost morale.
- Responsibility: Being trusted with more shows they're valued. Taking ownership of their work can be very motivating.
- Advancement and status: Knowing there's room to grow keeps them engaged. Promotions and recognition of their skills are great motivators.

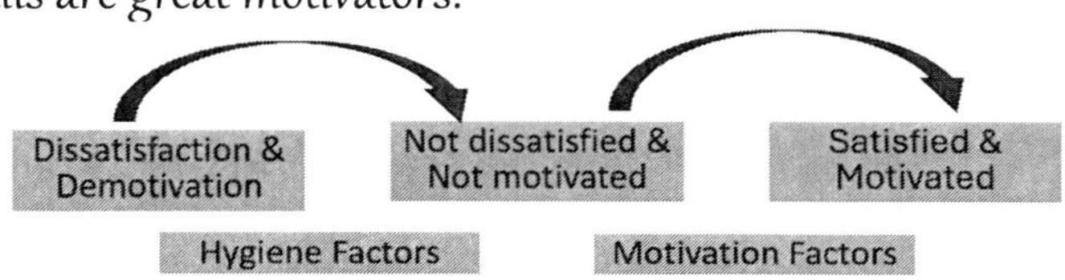

CHAPTER 15

Sharpen Your Communication Style

"The leaders' guide to getting heard"

Effective communication is essential, but many barriers can get in the way. One of the first barriers is mastering the language. This not only includes choosing the right words, but also using an appropriate tone, and being aware of body language. These are common challenges, but many people today are quite experts at navigating them, and a wealth of information is available on these topics. From a leader's point of view, sharp communication is effective because if the audience or the team does not understand it, the whole purpose is lost.

Imagine, you as a leader have devised a brilliant plan to boost your company's sales. You gather your team, full of excitement, and launch into your presentation. But as you speak, you notice disinterested expressions, drooping shoulders, and blank looks, and you quickly realise that your million-dollar idea has gone down the drain. This gets you thinking, what went wrong?

The answer lies in communication. Communication is not about gathering your team or delivering a speech; it is about connecting. Being a crucial aspect, a leader must have a communication style that acts as a bridge between you and the team or audience. If you are leading a team for instance, your communication should be clear, uncluttered, and interesting, so that your brilliant ideas and thoughts do not fall flat.

Just for your better understanding let's take Megha, a new team leader. her style of delivering instructions is extremely fast. She uses technical terminology where a simple word would actually do the work. This communication style may seem very stylish to her, but the fact of the matter is that a team does not understand anything. After the session when Megha asks for feedback, the responses are hesitant or non-existent. Why? Simply because her team feel lost and unheard. Her communication style may be very direct and crisp, but it is a barrier because the team members are eventually not even interested. Now here is where Megha has to brush up her skills and work on the communication part. Once she learns the correct style of communication, she will realise that her words are being heard and the team feels integral or important.

You see, effective communication is a two-way street. A leader's ability to tailor a message, and ensure clarity, creates a space for open dialogue. But how can a leader know the depth of effective communication?

There are three components of communication: Listening, Asking & Telling. Once a leader polishes these three aspects, he or she will effectively be able to motivate and inspire their teams and achieve remarkable things together.

From birth, we first learn to listen, then to ask questions, and finally to speak. However, as we grow, we tend to focus more on speaking and less on listening & asking. The problem is that most of us have practised telling more than listening or asking.

We need to create a balance between these three components, we should equally focus on Listening & Questioning too else can create concern. For example, during a conversation, we might be so eager to share our own experiences that we interrupt or talk over the other person, showing that we are not really listening. Or we might assume we know what the other person is going to say and respond before they've finished speaking.

In the upcoming chapters, we will cover these three components in detail to help you remove these barriers. We will explore how to listen effectively, how to ask the right questions, and how to communicate your thoughts and needs clearly. As part of the telling aspect, we will discuss how to share goals with your team, give constructive feedback, and manage conflicts. But before we do that, please remember, that communication is an ongoing process.

Communication that connects with people

You've probably heard sayings like

"Words can hurt you more than physical pain,"
"The wounds caused by hurtful words can take a lifetime to heal,"
"Be careful with words; once they are said, they can only be forgiven, not forgotten."

These emphasize the power of words and how they can impact others. We often hurt people with our words in several ways. One way is by passing judgmental statements. Another way is by communicating thoughts under the guise of sharing our feelings. Instead of expressing what we need, we often present an action plan and demand that it be followed. Let's dive deeper into these points to understand them better.

Be non-judgmental

Firstly, instead of sharing observations, we share our judgments or label people. This we have discussed in detail in earlier chapters. judgmental statements can create a barrier to effective communication because they can make others feel attacked or misunderstood. When we label or criticize someone, it can cause defensive reactions and shut down meaningful dialogue.

Separate out thoughts from your feelings.

Secondly, when we say we are sharing our feelings, we might actually be expressing opinions or judgments. For example, saying "I feel like you never listen to me" is more of a critique than a genuine expression of feelings. This can lead to misunderstandings and hurt feelings.

I have discussed in detail on how to identify and express your feelings in earlier chapter. Understand that beneath your emotion, lies your need. When you share your feelings, explain the underlying need. For example, instead of just saying "I'm upset", say, "I felt disappointed when you didn't come to the party. I was looking forward to celebrating it with you.". This slight play of direct words, the other person understands what you really wanted (to celebrate together) and can, therefore, respond with clarity.

Request your need instead of demanding some strategy

And the third aspect of sharing needs involves avoiding directing others with an action plan. For instance, instead of saying, "You need to start doing more work," which can sound controlling, we can express our needs rather directly. By sharing needs, we invite acceptance and understanding, making it easier for others to see why something needs to be done. This approach also keeps the conversation open for more collaborative solutions.

Another consideration is that of asking we tend to insist on actions, from others, which can lead to resistance and ill feelings. For example, stating, "You have to complete this today " might cause the other individual to feel pressured and undervalued. People are generally more willing to collaborate when they believe their perspectives and emotions are respected than just being instructed on what to do.

Combining these barriers helps clarify their impact. by requesting rather than demanding actions to fulfil our needs, we invite greater motivation and higher levels of energy from others. This approach encourages them to provide the best possible solutions, as they feel more valued and respected in the process.

To gain more clarity. Simply ask and listen!

To ensure clear communication, listen actively and encourage input. If any details are unclear, ask for clarification and use active listening to resolve doubts. Take feedback seriously and follow up with actions to show your commitment to understanding and addressing concerns.

Keep a check on the second-party emotion and body language

While delivering a session in front of a large audience or with your team, it's important to 'read the room' or in simpler words, gauge the emotions and body language of the listeners. This will help you in minutely analysing how well your communication is being perceived and allow you to adjust your approach, accordingly. For example, if you notice someone seemingly confused or apprehensive, you must pause to ask if there's anything that needs double clarification or additional explanation. This puts the audience at ease, and the comfort level aids the speaker and the audience to come in absolute sync.

Communication is not just having control over language and using the right tone/body language.

Three components of Language are Telling, Asking and Listening. We should focus on Listening and Asking more than telling. Listening and Asking helps you not only to clear some misunderstandings but also helps you to get some good suggestions/feedback to work upon.

To sharpen your communication style, follow the tips given below:

- Do not mix judgments with Observations
- Differentiate your feelings from your thoughts / opinions / judgements
- Take responsibility for your feelings and express your needs along with your feelings.
- Request a need instead of demanding strategy
- Clear out the context with team members

CHAPTER 16

Active Listening

"The unspoken power of great leaders."

Being a leader isn't just about listening; it's about actively listening. Active listening means paying close attention to what someone is saying, both verbally and non-verbally, and trying to understand their message to show the speakers that you care about what they have to say. Hearing is simply perceiving sounds, while listening is understanding the meaning behind those sounds. we actively listen, we can pick up on things that are not even said out loud, like someone's emotions or body language.

Active listening is a valuable skill that can improve your relationships and your effectiveness as a leader by following the steps you can become a better listener and reap the many benefits of active listening.

Active listening goes beyond the passive act of hearing words. It's a full-bodied engagement with the speaker, a keen attentiveness to everything they're saying and feeling, both verbally and through nonverbal cues. As a leader, this skill isn't a luxury - it's the cornerstone of building strong relationships, fostering a positive work environment, and ultimately, achieving success.

Imagine a workplace transformed into a place where employees feel truly heard and understood. Ideas flow freely, challenges are tackled collaboratively, and a deep sense of trust permeates every interaction. This isn't just a dream; it's the reality that active listening can cultivate for you and your team.

Consider the impact on your employees. When they feel like you genuinely care about their thoughts and concerns, they're more likely to be invested in their work. They become engaged, motivated, and willing to push themselves further. Active listening demonstrates that their input is valued, creating a safe space for open communication. This free flow of ideas fuels better problem-solving, sparks innovation, and leads to a team that consistently performs at its peak.

So, how do you transform yourself into an active listener?

Give a 100% to listening: To become an active listener, it's crucial to be fully present in the moment. This means giving your employees your undivided attention. Start by silencing your phone, pushing distractions aside, and focusing solely on the conversation at hand.
It's also important to set aside your agenda and approach the conversation with an open mind.

Avoid Taking Things Personally: One key aspect of active listening is to avoid taking things personally. When you take things personally, you blend your thoughts and assessments with the speaker's words.

Do not judge the speaker or ideas: Instead of judging the speaker or their ideas, acknowledge their feelings and summarize what they've said. This demonstrates that you're actively engaged and following along.

Listening to Different Elements: As an active listener, it's essential to listen for facts, feelings, intentions, or needs. By doing so, you gain a deeper understanding of the speaker's perspective.

Ask question, if you need more clarity: If something seems unclear, don't hesitate to ask questions to clarify and ensure that you're on the same page.

Therefore, active listening is a valuable skill that can greatly enhance communication and relationships. By being fully present, avoiding personal biases, and listening for various elements, you can transform yourself into an active listener who truly understands and connects with others.

Here are some common hurdles to good listening:

- Thinking you already know everything. This can prevent you from being open to new ideas.
- Judging the speaker. This can make the speaker feel different and less likely to share openly
- Trying to fix the speaker's problems. sometimes people just need to be heard not fixed
- Getting distracted. Put your phone away and avoid multitasking when you're listening to someone.
- Diverting or directing the speaker's point of view
- Intruding upon the speaker's pace
- Creating and responding to distractions, ruining the flow and connectivity of the context
- Trying to give an influenced comment, trying to defy the speaker
- Responding before the speaker finish their thoughts

The Benefits of Active Listening

Next, it's important to take a step back and understand why active listening matters.

- **Active** listening demonstrates the value placed on others' opinions and fosters a sense of inclusion and respect.
- It facilitates understanding between individuals or teams, which is crucial for building strong relationships.
- Active listening builds psychological safety, encouraging people to share their perspectives and creating a sense of belonging.

- It enhances coaching effectiveness by allowing for a deeper understanding of issues and synchronisation.
- Demonstrating active listening sets an example for others, establishing a culture where everyone feels heard and valued.

By mastering active listening, you become more than just a leader; you become a conductor, drawing out the best in your team and creating a symphony of success. You cultivate an environment where employees feel valued, respected, and empowered to do their best work. This, in turn, propels your organization towards a brighter future, brimming with innovation and productivity. So, the next time someone starts talking, remember, that it's not just about hearing their words; it's about listening to the potential and possibilities they hold within them.

Listen to the life stories of team members

A leader should make it a point to listen to their team members' life stories at least once a month. This practice helps in developing active listening skills and provides valuable insights into the team members' backgrounds. Understanding their stories can help the leader better understand their behaviors and motivations.

Active listening is key for leaders to connect with their teams. It means, fully focusing on what's said and what's unsaid, showing they care, and encouraging open communication.

The key components of active listening are:

- *Release your agenda and give 100% to listening. Listening is different from hearing.*

- Be Attentive, maintain eye contact, be sensitive to inconsistency in the speaker's verbal and nonverbals
- Amplify what you listen, ask clarifying question and encourage other to continue
- Reflect what you listened: Paraphrasing what speakers shared, summarize what you understand
- Prevents judgement, encourages openness
- Avoids personalisation, stays objective

Some of key benefits of active listening are:

- Builds understanding, strengthens relationships
- Values opinions, fosters respect
- Creates psychological safety, cultivates belonging

CHAPTER 17

GROW (Asking Powerful Questions)

"Asking rather than telling, creates space"

Imagine, your team member is stuck in a maze. One of the options is you give them the solution, but as a leader you know it is not good this way, your team should find the solution on their own. That's where the GROW model comes in. It's like a flashlight that you can use to show the path to your team members without actually giving any solution.

The GROW model stands for Goal, Reality, Options, and Way Forward. It is a powerful tool for leaders to help their team members set and achieve their goals. Here's how it works:

- **Goal:** As a leader, guide your team members to identify specific and achievable goals. Encourage them to be clear and specific about what they want to achieve, whether it's a project milestone, professional development target, or personal growth objective.
- **Reality:** Help team members assess their current situation objectively. Encourage them to identify their strengths, resources, and any challenges they may face. This step is crucial for creating a realistic plan to achieve their desired goals.
- **Options:** Brainstorm with your team members to explore different paths and solutions. Encourage them to think creatively and consider alternative approaches to overcome obstacles. As a leader, provide support and guidance, but let them take ownership of finding the best way forward.
- **Way Forward:** Work with your team members to develop a concrete plan of action. Help them break down their goals into manageable steps and set deadlines. Encourage them to identify ways to measure progress and stay motivated throughout the process.

By using the GROW Model, you empower your team members to find their own solutions and take ownership of their development. As a leader, you play the role of a support system or supportive guide, asking powerful questions that help them unlock their potential and become winners by achieving their goals.

How can someone provide guidance to team members without dictating their actions?
Here's the secret sauce: powerful questions. These are not your typical "yes or no" questions. They are open-ended and thought-provoking, prompting you to dig deep and discover your own answers. Imagine questions like "What would success look like for you?" or "What resources do you already have that can help you?"

As a leader, mastering the GROW Model can transform the way you guide and empower your team. This four-step system is a powerful tool for setting and achieving goals, allowing you to ask questions that lead your team members to find their own solutions. Unlike traditional leadership approaches that rely on giving advice or directions, the GROW Model focuses on smooth self-discovery and promoting ownership.

The GROW model is a powerful tool not just for professional settings, but for anyone looking to achieve their goals. Whether you're a manager leading your team or a student tackling a challenging project, GROW can help you chart your course and reach your destination. So, the next time you're feeling lost, remember that sometimes the best solutions come from within, and all you need is a little guidance to find them.

Keys to success

The success of the GROW Model hinges on two main factors: the ability to ask powerful questions and the practice of active listening. Powerful questions stimulate deep thinking and self-reflection, while active listening ensures that your team members feel heard and understood.

Sample questions for each phase

GOAL

- What specific goals are you trying to achieve?
- What do you want to change?
- What outcome do you want to see?

REALITY

- How far are you from achieving your goal?"
- What do you need to do that you aren't doing now?"
- Is this the right goal for you?
- Do you have the necessary skills, resources, etc.?

OBSTACLES OR OPTIONS

- How could you do things differently?
- What options exist to help achieve your goal?
- What will specifically change once you achieve your goal?

WAY FORWARD

- How committed are you to reaching your goal (use a 1-10 scale)?
- How will you know when you've achieved your goal?

THINGS TO AVOID

To maximise the effectiveness of the GROW Model, avoid the following pitfalls:

- Judging: Don't judge whether someone is doing something right or wrong, as this can bias your questions.
- "Why" Questions: Avoid "why" questions, as they can imply judgment.

- Giving Suggestions: Don't give suggestions or express agreement/disagreement, as this can limit the other person's brainstorming.
- Ask Open-Ended Questions: Encourage the person to understand their emotions and needs, which can help them find the best strategies and action plans.

DISTINCTIVENESS OF THE GROW MODEL

The GROW Model is unique because it helps people find their own solutions rather than providing advice. this makes it distinct from counselling, mentoring, or teaching. The mantra here is: "Say less, ask more."

Benefits of using the GROW Model

Even if you are not a subject matter expert, you can use the GROW Model to help team members plan tasks independently. This approach has several benefits:

1. **Ownership and commitment:** Considering that in the GROW Model, a leader has not given any suggestions/inputs, but has asked powerful questions. This gives an edge and liberty to the team/audience to propose a solution, and this led to an increased ownership and commitment.
2. **New ideas:** The possibility of the team members brimming with new and out-of-the-box ideas is a sign that the model has stamped its effective impact on their minds. Once they reach this stage, there is scope for wider horizons and larger perspectives.
3. **Enhanced learning:** It is an undoubted fact that once the above two aspects are on the go, the scope for enhanced learning begins. and this enhanced or greater learning that comes along with high confidence, is not just for the team members but also for that one person who leads them throughout the journey. The leader achieves a different

level of confidence that makes her/him improve and gear up for the next level, only to share it with team members as and when the time is ripe.

More on powerful questioning

Powerful questions are a cornerstone of the GROW Model. they should reflect active listening and show that you understand the person's perspective. here are some key aspects:

- Reflect Active Listening: Show you're listening by paraphrasing. Examples:
    - Can you tell me more about...?
    - What did you mean by...?
- Presume Positive Intent: Affirm effort, skills, integrity, and commitment. Examples:
    - What are you planning to...?
    - How are you going to...?
- Evoke Discovery, Insight, Commitment, or Action: Encourage the person to gain insight or act. Examples:
    - What would you do if...?
    - What were you thinking when...?
    - How can you apply...?
- Challenge Current Assumptions: Push the person to consider their patterns or assumptions. Examples:
    - How else might you...?
    - What is stopping you from...?
    - What would happen if...?
- Create Greater Clarity: Help the person find clarity or look at something in a new way. Examples
    - What do you think it means...?
    - Help me understand what you mean by...?
    - What will you learn from this...?
- Move the Person Toward Their Goals: Help the person take action, set goals, and get the help they need. Examples:
    - What do you want to learn?

- What have you tried so far?
- What kind of help will you need?

All you readers must understand how powerful a tool like the GROW Model can be. It helps you guide your team to find their own solutions. By asking the right questions, you can encourage deep thinking and self-discovery. This model fosters ownership and commitment. it also promotes creativity and learning.

As we conclude, here are the take-aways.
Remember to:

- Focus on goals
- Understand the current reality.
- Explore obstacles and options
- Plan the way forward

Avoid jumping or giving advice. Instead, listen actively and ask open-minded questions. this approach builds confidence and promotes growth.

Therefore, by using the GROW Model, you can lead you and your team to success. Empower them to achieve their goal and watch them thrive.

CHAPTER 18

Setting SMART Goals

"Setting goals is the first step in turning the invisible into the visible"

Keeping the corporate world in mind, how does one define smartness?
Be it a manager or a team member, how can they ascertain that they are smart?

Often, we have found ourselves dissatisfied and unhappy with our work profile. There are times when we keep hopping from one job to the other, trying to be the best fit. We may be working hard, and pushing ourselves to outshine others just to prove we are the best, but it does not work. This situation applies to a manager, a leader, or a team member because we have all gone through this stage in our lives.

But worry no more because the contents of this chapter will allow you to look yourself in the mirror and forge ahead with complete positivity. Yes, the tables are about to turn!

Let us dive in and understand the **SMART** guide.

SMART is an acronym that can be used to define the goal(s) for self or team members. To ensure goals are clear and attainable, the following should be understood and integrated:

- **S**pecific (simple, sensible, significant).
  What will you achieve? What will you do?
- **M**easurable (meaningful, motivating).
  What data will you use to decide whether you've met the goal?
- **A**chievable (agreed, attainable).

Are you sure you can do this? Do you have the right skills and resources?

- **R**elevant (reasonable, realistic resourced, results-based). Does the goal align with those of your team or organization? How will the result matter?
- **Time-bound** (time-based, time-limited, time/cost limited, timely, time-sensitive). What is the deadline for accomplishing the goal?

Time to get SMART!

Let me take some examples here.

On the face of it, the below goals may seem kind of ok, but if you look closely, they are simply baseless:

- I want to read more
- I need to get organised
- I want to learn to cook

Where is the clarity? This leads to the following three sins of goal setting:

1. Unspecified - You may say you want to "read more," but what does that really mean? When will you do it? How will you do it?
2. Unrealistic - You want to get organised, but what is the course of action that you intend to take?
3. Reliance on willpower over systems - It's great that you want to learn to cook, but are you even aware of the POA that you will need? Do you have a strategy in mind?

Now Let me make these goals SMART

Terrible Goal	Bad Goal	SMART Goal
I want to read more	I want to read 5 books	Starting today, I will read for 30 minutes every night before bed for the next 3 months

Terrible Goal	Bad Goal	SMART Goal
I need to get organized	I want to declutter my house	Every Saturday for the next 2 months, I will spend 2 hours organizing one room in my house
I want to learn to cook	I want to cook 10 new recipes	Starting this week, I will cook one new recipe every Wednesday evening for the next 10 weeks

Therefore, SMART goals provide a remedy for indistinct, directionless New Year's resolution goals. Setting goals cannot be done at the spur of the moment before the clock strikes 12! They must be planned cautiously and with a fresh mindset.

By making your goals specific, measurable, achievable, relevant, and time-bound, you'll be able to establish the foundation for achievement. This will avoid common traps of unclear and impractical goals.

Now we will dig deeper and refer to the "checklist" for writing a SMART goal or objective.

1. **SPECIFIC**: Define the exact outcome you aim for.
    - What will you achieve?
    - Envision the details of your goal. What do you see when you picture yourself working towards it?
    - What is the specific action step?
2. **MEASURABLE**: How will I know I've accomplished the goal?
   There are different levels of "reading" or "cooking." Avoid words that may have unclear meanings like, "learn" or "feel" since you can't measure them. Instead, use action verbs like

"read," "cook," or "organise." Then, turn those words into tangible metrics.

The questions you can ask yourself:

- How will you determine completion?
- What are some measurable milestones you can achieve?
- Can someone else recognize when it's finished?
- Is it quantifiable?

3. **ATTAINABLE:** Mentors often discuss Tiny Habits - small actions that initiate our journey to success. The most effective way to reach a goal is to make it incredibly easy for your future self to take the right actions. For example, someone has set a goal to reduce weight and stay fit. They claim to jog for five days a week. So, instead of committing to run or jog five days a week, start with one day and progress gradually.
   - Are the necessary resources available to achieve the objective?
   - Do you require a reading club, a cooking course, or attend a workshop on 'how to stay organised?
   - Am I prepared to pursue this even when motivation is lacking?
   - Are there any time or financial constraints that need consideration? Am I aiming too high to begin with? (Remember, you can always increase the intensity of your goal later on.)

4. **RELEVANT**: Is this a priority in my life right now? Question yourself, do you really want to do it, and do you even care about doing it, or are you just setting this goal because you got influenced by a friend or colleague who was very well-organised, or a great cook, and so on?

So, you place a sticky note on your worktable that has many other notes, you know, work-related. And it was only after a couple of weeks that you found this sticky note under the table! That's when it struck me and I realised the truth, that was, that it was not relevant and important to me anymore. When I acknowledged that I wasn't going to do it, at least not soon, I felt a sense of relief. This relief helped me regain my focus on what was it that I wanted to do now.

The questions that liberated me and brought me on track:

- Why am I doing this?
- Is this a priority for me?
- Will I be able to accomplish all the other goals in my life?

5. **TIME-ORIENTED:** Set a deadline to reassess your goal and mark it on your calendar. Re-evaluate the goals periodically to ensure they are still achievable and relevant. The following questions should be very clear:
   - When will the goal be completed?
   - Have I set a deadline?
   - Have I marked it on the calendar?
   - Will I know in three months, if I'm on the right track?

The benefits of SMART Goal are:

1. SMART goals eliminate ambiguity, enabling clear determination of whether a goal has been met or not.
2. They are time-bound, allowing progress to be measured against specific deadlines, indicating if the goal was met or not.
3. The framework fosters accountability, reducing the likelihood of making excuses for goals not being met.

4. SMART goals facilitate constructive feedback by defining criteria for success and distinguishing between good job done and bad job done.

A leader or a manager has to have the thoughts and concepts clear because now it's time to share them with the team. The SMART goal concept, once shared with the team, will be a step up for each individual as a human being and as an asset to the organisation. Beyond any doubt, the road ahead is indeed going to be very SMART!

Setting SMART goals is crucial for success in the corporate world. It ensures clarity, measurability, accountability, and effective feedback. By defining Specific, Measurable, Achievable, Relevant, and Time-bound goals, individuals can set clear objectives and track their progress effectively. This approach helps avoid common pitfalls like ambiguity, unrealistic expectations, and reliance on willpower. Overall, SMART goals provide a framework for strategic goal setting that leads to improved performance and satisfaction in work.

CHAPTER 19

Sharing Feedback

"Delivering a feedback is a must-have skill"

Effective feedback is the foundation of building a high-performance team. It's a two-way street that allows leaders to recognise and celebrate accomplishments, while also offering constructive criticism to help team members improve.

Sharing feedback is a positive assurance that motivates individuals and creates a happy culture of continuous learning. By creating a safe space for open communication, feedback empowers team members to share ideas, learn from each other's experiences, and collectively and confidently, refine processes, fuelling innovation, and reaching their full potential.

So, the first and foremost question that pops up:
What Kind of Manager do **YOU** want to be?

1. Tough manager – Focussed on boosting profits, often at the cost of employee morale. This type of manager prioritises financial results above all, which can lead to a stressed and unhappy team.
2. Soft Manager – Prioritises staff happiness, sometimes at the expense of company profits. this manager values employee satisfaction highly, which can sometimes result in lower financial progress.
3. Top performing manager – Achieves top results while keeping a positive work environment and availability for the team members. This manager balances success and well-being, creating a productive and happy workplace. Not just an asset to the company, who effectively drives the team but also has earned the trust and faith of the team members.

Setting goals and having a solid feedback system are crucial for building a high-performing team. The first step towards an effective feedback system is getting clear expectations, and SMART Goals help leaders outline what is expected from each team member. We have already covered goal setting in the previous chapter.

In this chapter, we will explore what, when, and how to share feedback.

First, let's Focus on **how to share feedback.**
Sharing feedback is essential. While positive feedback is easier to give, it's crucial to learn how to deliver constructive criticism effectively.

The REACH model of feedback is a comprehensive approach that can significantly impact how feedback is given and received. In this model, communication is key, as it aims to address behaviour or actions constructively while maintaining a positive relationship between the giver and receiver of feedback.

Real-Time Feedback: Providing feedback promptly is crucial. Delayed feedback may lose its effectiveness and relevance. For instance, if a team member consistently arrives late, addressing this behaviour immediately can prevent it from becoming a recurring issue. By doing so, you demonstrate that you are attentive to performance and committed to addressing concerns promptly. Regular, ongoing feedback is more effective than infrequent, annual reviews. Continuous communication allows for timely adjustments and improvements. For example, if a team member consistently meets their deadlines, acknowledging and appreciating this achievement immediately reinforces positive behaviour and motivates continued performance.

Explain Intentions: Clearly stating the purpose of feedback sets the stage for a productive conversation. This ensures that both parties are aligned in understanding the feedback's objective. For instance, if a team member's work quality has been inconsistent, explaining that the goal is to help them improve and grow in their role can make the feedback more constructive and less confrontational.

Action-Oriented Focus on the specific actions or behaviours that need improvement, rather than making generalized or personal critiques. Providing concrete examples helps the receiver understand what they need to change. For instance, instead of saying, "You're not a team player," you could say, "During the last team project, you didn't collaborate effectively, as seen when you didn't contribute to the group discussions.

Consequences: Ask the receiver, what are the consequences. This will help the receiver understand the consequences of their actions. This encourages them to reflect on their behaviour and its impact. For example, if a team member's constant tardiness is affecting team meetings, discussing how their behaviour affects team productivity can help them see the importance of being punctual.

Offer **Help** & have a **Handshake:** Offer support and assistance but allow the receiver to take ownership of finding solutions. This empowers them to address the issues themselves, leading to more sustainable change. For example, if a team member is struggling with a particular task, offering to provide additional training or resources shows your commitment to their development.

In the end, pause for a moment to let them feel your appreciation/ reprimand. In case of appreciation, encourage them to continue their good work and show your support with a handshake or a supportive gesture. And in case of reprimand, allow a moment of silence to let them reflect. then, show that you are on their side with a handshake or supportive gesture. Remind them of their value but be clear that their performance in this instance was not acceptable. Realize them that when the reprimand is over, it's over.

What and When to Share Feedback

The mode and frequency of feedback are crucial considerations. Whenever you notice someone doing something good or making a mistake, that's the time to provide feedback. According to the REACH model, feedback should be immediate and in real-time.

The two key benefits of immediate feedback are:

1. It is easy to relate what happened. Generally, with time, people tend to forget the exact scenario. If we share immediate feedback, it is easy to recall what happened and what was the cause.
2. On getting prompt feedback, the team member will get to the task almost immediately. On the other side, if the feedback is delayed for a monthly review, the reoccurrence of the same situation is highly probable.

It's important to share both positive and negative feedback.

Negative feedback is essential for growth and improvement. It helps individuals understand areas where they need to improve and guides how to do better. By balancing both positive and negative feedback, you create a supportive environment where everyone can thrive. You might wonder why positive feedback is necessary. Sharing positive feedback serves 2 purposes:

1. When you acknowledge positive actions. it motivates the recipient to continue performing well. This recognition helps individuals reach their full potential by identifying and appreciating their good work.
2. If you later need to provide negative feedback, the recipient is less likely to feel that their efforts are only criticised. Having received praise in the past, they will be more open to constructive criticism.

Here are a few tips to make your feedback more effective:

1. Be specific about the problem/issue, avoiding generic statements like, "You always do this."
2. Never be sarcastic, as sarcasm obscures the importance and relevance of what went wrong and causes confusion along with embarrassment for the team member. Such a manager/leader staunchly believes in a famous Hindi proverb, "सांप भी मर गया और लाठी भी नहीं टूटी" which translates to,' The snake (problem) died but the stick (the team member) did not break. but it turns out just the opposite "सांप भी नहीं मरता और लाठी भी टूट जाती है" which simply means that the problem (snake) isn't handled and the stick (team member) breaks.
3. When giving negative feedback, we should focus on 'what is wrong' rather than 'who is wrong'. It is important to shift our discussion from feedback to feed forward. By feed forward, I mean we should spend less time dwelling on what went wrong and more time discussing what we expect in the future. What's done is done; Let's learn from it and strive to do our best moving forward.
4. When discussing consequences instead of simply stating them we should adopt a coaching approach and ask the recipient to identify the outcome themselves. By asking relevant questions, we help the recipient understand the repercussions.

In the case of negative feedback, the consequences are inherently negative. If you just tell the recipient, they may feel hurt. However, if they articulate the consequences themselves, the negativity is reduced and their acceptance of the feedback increases.

What if you do not share the feedback

Let us understand the repercussions of not providing or sharing feedback.

Say, for instance, a team member has displayed good performance most of the time. But now a lag is being witnessed. This is where the leader gets a little apprehensive about whether he/she should give feedback or not. At this point, the leader expands the thought process and gets more involved in the team member's supervision, and day-to-day work.

While this may seem a good pattern, the flip side of it is the loop where losing the trust factor and various other aspects begin to get stuck.

Let's do a step-by-step analysis of the same of the above-mentioned case scenario.

Leader: increases supervision and becomes more involved.

Team member: interprets it as a lack of trust and confidence.

Becomes anxious and begins to doubt his/her own ability and thought process.

Becomes hesitant to make decisions and the motivation to perform, decreases.

Leader: at this point, the leader is able to affirm the decrease in performance.

And that is where the leader considerably escalates the supervision.

Team member: feels constantly being scrutinised and judged negatively

Team member: Ultimately, the team member loses the management's trust and plans to look for other job options.

This example demonstrates that not sharing feedback or failing to act on it, can create confusion. Therefore, it is crucial to provide feedback promptly.

Create a gratitude culture by saying thank you with slips, verbal acknowledgements, and other small gestures. This fosters goodwill and supportive work management and positive work environment.

The REACH Model of feedback emphasises timely, constructive communication aimed at addressing behaviour or actions positively. It advocates for ***real-time feedback*** *to prevent issues from escalating and encourages ongoing, consistent communication for continuous improvement. Clearly* ***explaining intentions, focusing on actions*** *rather than personal traits, and discussing* ***consequences*** *help the receiver comprehend the purpose of the feedback and its impact. Offering* ***support and assistance*** *while allowing the receiver to take ownership of solutions empowers them to make lasting changes and positive impacts.*

CHAPTER 20

Conflict Management & How to Say No

"In the middle of conflict lies opportunity

Every organisation experience conflict. It's understandable that when two people are involved, there will certainly be a different perspective on any given situation, which can increase the chances of disagreement. But why do we have conflicts, and is it good to have them? Addressing workplace conflict is crucial because ignoring it doesn't make it vanish. Unresolved conflicts can lead to missed deadlines, growing resentment, and failed projects.

Conflicts may arise from differences in perspectives, expectations, beliefs, and values. Sometimes, it's just about having different information. Conflict can be a positive force for innovation and improvement when managed well. However, if ignored, it can become destructive. Pretending conflict doesn't exist won't make it go away. Ignoring issues can be disastrous.
When a conflict arises, people generally react in three ways: aggressively, assertively, or submissively. Aggressive reactions involve pushing for one's own rights at the expense of others' rights. Submissive reactions involve giving in to others' rights while ignoring one's own. Understanding these reactions can help in choosing the best approach to manage conflict.

Conflicts can escalate through various stages:

1. Emergence: is when the conflict starts to become noticeable.
2. Escalation: is when the conflict intensifies & becomes serious.
3. Tension: is when the conflict causes significant stress & strain.
4. Crisis: is when the conflict reaches a peak and needs urgent resolution.

Behaviours in conflicts can be overt or covert. Overt behaviour is visible and apparent actions or verbal expressions, while covert ones are hidden and concealed with differences that are not openly discussed. Understanding whether a conflict is overt, or covert can help in addressing it appropriately.
Imagine a scenario where two colleagues have a disagreement. Their differing perspectives can be a breeding ground for conflict. To effectively manage these situations, organisations can leverage a decision-making concept.
Let us dive straight into it.

The conflict resolution grid
This consists of two key factors:

1. Importance of the task: How critical is achieving the specific objective? This defines how assertive are you?
2. Importance of relationship: How important is maintaining a positive working relationship between the individuals involved? This defines how cooperative you are?

Choosing your approach
There are five main approaches to conflict management:

Avoiding: As the term suggests, ignoring the conflict or avoiding it is like putting the whole situation on hold. The process of postponing may not be the best solution in the given scenario.

Accommodate: When preserving the relationship is essential, even if it means putting the goal aside temporarily, then accommodation is best. Imagine a situation where a new team member needs support; an experienced colleague might prioritise offering help over immediate completion of a task.

Compete: If the goal is paramount and the relationship is less important, a more assertive approach (competing) might be necessary. This should be handled firmly but respectfully. Think of a situation with a tight deadline; clear and direct communication might be required to ensure completion.

Compromise: Finding common ground is key when both the goal and the relationship hold weight. This (compromising) could involve concessions from both parties/teams/individuals. Negotiating a revised deadline or slightly modified approach to a project can be an example of compromise.

Collaborate: When both the goals and the relationship are crucial, collaboration is ideal. This involves working together to find a solution that benefits both parties. Imagine a project requiring expertise from both colleagues; brainstorming together can lead to a more innovative outcome.

These approaches can be seen on a scale from assertiveness (concern for self) to cooperativeness (concern for others). After understanding all of the above, it is clear there's no one-size-fits-all solution. The ideal approach depends on the specific conflict situation. By understanding these different approaches and utilizing the decision-making tool, organisations can foster a more collaborative and productive work environment.

Let me explain this in a simple and fun manner:

Analysis of Conflict Management Styles

The image illustrates various conflict management styles, categorized by their levels of concern for relationships and outcomes. Here's a detailed analysis:

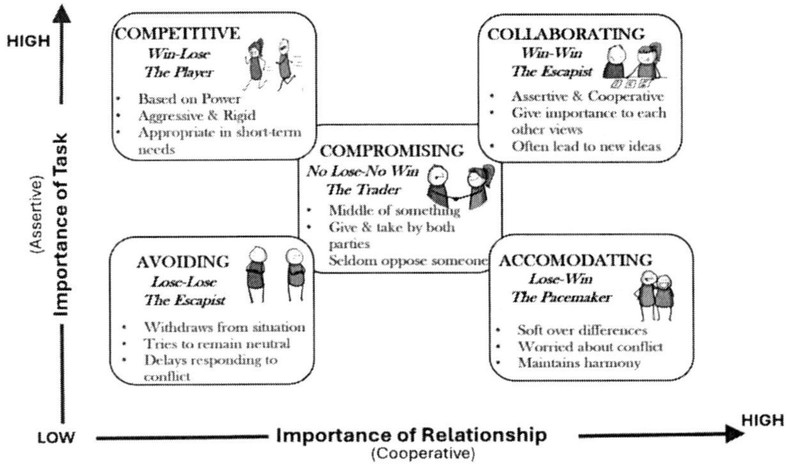

Avoidance (Lose-Lose)
Nickname: The Escapist
Characteristics:

- Withdraws from the situation.
- Tries to remain neutral.
- Delays responding to conflict.

Usage: Avoidance might be used when the conflict is trivial or when there are more pressing issues. However, it can result in unresolved problems and lost opportunities.

Accommodation (Lose-Win)
Nickname: The Peacemaker
Characteristics:

- Suppresses and smooths over differences.
- Dreads conflict.
- Maintains harmony.

Usage: This style is often used when maintaining relationships is more important than achieving immediate outcomes. It helps to preserve peace but may lead to unresolved issues.

Competition (Win-Lose)
Nickname: The Player
Characteristics:

- Based on power.
- Aggressive and uncooperative.
- Appropriate for short-term needs.

Usage: This style is effective when quick, decisive action is needed. It prioritizes outcomes over relationships and can be beneficial in competitive environments but may damage relationships.

Compromise (No Lose-No Win)
Nickname: The Trader
Characteristics:

- Middle-of-the-road position.
- Give and take by both parties.
- Seldom confronts conflict directly.

Usage: Compromise is suitable when a quick, mutually acceptable solution is needed. It involves each party giving up something, leading to moderate satisfaction.

Collaboration (Win-Win)
Nickname: The Problem-Solver
Characteristics:

- Assertive and cooperative.
- Objectively evaluates differing views.
- Often leads to creativity and new ideas.

Usage: This approach is ideal when both relationships and outcomes are important. It seeks solutions that satisfy all parties, promoting innovation and lasting agreements.

Understanding these conflict management styles helps in choosing the right approach based on the situation. Balancing concern for relationships and outcomes is key to effective conflict resolution. Accommodating and avoiding may preserve relationships but often leave issues unresolved. Competing ensures outcomes but can harm relationships. Compromising offers a middle ground while collaborating seeks the best of both worlds, fostering innovation and mutual satisfaction.

How to collaborate to reach to a common solution

The conflict management aspect is complete with a vital tool or guideline. Expressing disagreement constructively is essential for effective communication in the workplace.

In the previous chapter on communication skills, we discussed that focusing on following four traits, helps you communicate in a way that will not hurt the other person

1) Observation, not the judgments
2) Feeling, not the thoughts
3) Needs, not strategy
4) Request, not the demand

When we are in conflict, if both the parties share their thoughts with four above points, it will help them to understand each other in better way and reach to a common collaborative solution.

Along the same lines, there are four-step methods to collaborate in case of a conflict. The Describe, Explain, Specify, and Conclude method is a simple and effective way to achieve this. By following these four steps, you can address issues without causing unnecessary conflict and work toward a resolution everyone can agree on.

Describe: State the facts without judgment.

Example: "The machine needs repair, and production is scheduled soon."

Explain: Share your feelings using "I" statements.
Example: "I feel stressed because I'm responsible for delays."

Specify: Suggest ways to address the issue.
Example: "Can you prioritize repairing the machine so production can continue?"

Conclude: Agree on a solution.
Example: "Let's ensure the repair is done quickly to meet the deadlines."

The above method helps both the parties to express disagreements clearly and constructively, leading to effective problem-solving and better workplace communication.

Effective conflict management involves a clear, three-step process: listening, asking, and telling. By following these steps, you can navigate disagreements more constructively and foster better understanding and resolution.

Listen

The first step in conflict management is to listen. This involves giving your full attention to the person speaking, without interrupting or planning your response while they are talking. By genuinely listening, you show respect and empathy, which can help de-escalate the situation. It allows you to understand their perspective and feelings, paving the way for a more constructive dialogue. This approach can be particularly effective in personal relationships, where misunderstandings often stem from a lack of proper communication.

Ask

After listening, the next step is to ask questions. Clarify any points that are unclear and seek to understand the underlying issues. Asking open-ended questions can help the other person express their thoughts and feelings more fully. This step is crucial because it shows that you are actively engaged in finding a resolution and value their input. In my own experience, asking thoughtful questions has often led to uncovering deeper issues that were not immediately apparent, leading to more effective problem-solving.

Tell

The final step is to tell your side of the story. Share your perspective calmly and respectfully, ensuring that your words are clear and concise. It's important to communicate your feelings and thoughts without placing blame or becoming defensive. By doing so, you can foster a more collaborative environment where both parties feel heard and respected. In my past relationships, I found that when I expressed myself honestly and calmly, it helped to build trust and understanding, even during conflict.

How to Say NO

Sometimes, you need to say no to someone. Saying no is a type of conflict, so what you've learned about handling conflicts applies here. Following are some specific tips to help you say no effectively:

1. Be kind and polite: some people worry about seeming rude or unhelpful when they say no. If you respond to quickly or bluntly, it can come across as harsh. However, saying no can be done gracefully and kindly, which can make your message easier to accept.
2. Give your reasons: Offer a brief explanation without expressing opinions. Share the facts and your feelings so the

other person knows you are not neglecting them but are simply unavailable.

3. Understand their needs and suggest alternatives: Show that you understand their needs and, if possible, refer them to a different strategy or suggest an alternative timeline.
4. Keep the door open: Maintain good relationships by not burning bridges when you decline. Keeping the door open for future opportunities is important for career growth.

By following these tips, you can say no in a way that is respectful and keeps your relationships intact.

Understand the Causes of Conflict: Recognize that conflicts arise from differences in perspectives, expectations, beliefs, values, and information.

Address Conflict Promptly: Ignoring conflicts can lead to bigger problems. Tackle issues head-on to maintain a healthy work environment.

Recognize Reaction Styles: People react to conflict in aggressive, assertive, or submissive ways. Knowing these can help in managing conflicts effectively.

Identify Conflict Levels: Conflicts can escalate through emergence, escalation, tension, and crisis. Early intervention can prevent crises.

Distinguish Overt and Covert Behaviours: Overt conflicts are visible, while covert conflicts are hidden. Address both to ensure all issues are resolved.

Use Different Conflict Management Approaches: Avoiding, accommodating , competing, compromising, and collaborating are key strategies. Choose the right approach based on the situation.

Describe, Explain, Specify, and Conclude helps in expressing disagreements constructively.

Listen, Ask, tell: A very effective construction to take care of conflict management.

Learn to Say No Politely: Be polite and considerate, provide reasons without debate, keep future possibilities open, and suggest alternatives when declining requests.

These takeaways emphasize the importance of understanding, addressing, and managing conflicts effectively. Applying these principles can lead to a more productive and harmonious workplace. Knowing how to say no gracefully ensures that you maintain professional relationships while managing your responsibilities.

Something not right does not mean it is wrong...

Rajesh Sachdev

About the Author

I have 30 years of corporate experience, and I was fortunate enough to engage in leadership roles that gave me a fresh new understanding of becoming a better leader. My undying passion was to give back to society through the learnings that I had accumulated.
To fulfil my passion, I planned to become a full-time facilitator for leadership development and coaching.

My career commenced with the role of a Software Engineer, and I gradually assisted my upward growth to the capacity of Resourcing Head in a CMMi-Level 5 IT company. Successfully headed a team of 200+ IT professionals and eventually landed a prestigious position as HR Head with the pioneers in IIT-JEE coaching institutes (Pan India) based in New Delhi.

I have had the opportunity to deal with a lot of people throughout my career and my passion to understand the human psyche urged me to translate this vast knowledge into conveyable strategies.

My intellectual bent always pushed me to read idealistic books and this undying devotedness urged me to help people attain their highest and truest version. And that's when I started to facilitate the same through books and training programs on leadership.